SEWING
FOR
PLUS SIZES

Creating Clothes
that Fit & Flatter

Barbara Deckert

The Taunton Press

Cover photos by Jack Deutsch

The Taunton Press
Inspiration for hands-on living®

Publisher: Jim Childs

Acquisitions Editor: Jolynn Gower

Editorial Assistant: Sarah Coe

Copy Editor: Nancy N. Bailey

Designer: Amy Russo

Layout Artist: Suzie Yannes

Photographers: Jack Deutsch, Susan Kahn

Hair and Makeup: Cheryl Calo

Illustrators: Bob La Pointe and Shawn Banner

Indexer: Lynda Stannard

Sewing for Plus Sizes was originally published
in hardcover in 1999 by The Taunton Press, Inc.

The Taunton Press, Inc., 63 South Main Street,
Newtown, CT 06470-2344
e-mail: tp@taunton.com

Library of Congress Cataloging-in-Publication Data

Deckert, Barbara.
    Sewing for plus sizes: design, fit, and construction for ample apparel/Barbara Deckert.
        p.   cm.
        ISBN 978-1-56158-551-9
    1. Machine sewing. 2. Tailoring (Women's) 3. Overweight women—Costume. I.
Title
    TT713.D37 1999   99-12287
    646.4'04—dc21   CIP

Printed in the United States of America

15 14 13 12 11 10 9

To my husband, Gerry, for his support and assistance, and to my plus-sized children, Brian and Claire.

contents

introduction

Every once in a while, as I'm racing through my local mall to the sewing store, some stranger stops me, compliments my outfit, and asks me where I bought it. I'm always flabbergasted when this happens because the stranger is always thin to average in build, while I wear about a size 32. Sometimes Bad Barbara wants to come out and reply, "Honey, it doesn't come in your size," but then Good Barbara prevails and offers the woman a business card.

For a variety of reasons, the ready-to-wear industry has failed to meet even our most basic clothing needs. Once, while checking the directory at the same mall, a gentleman asked me which shops sold plus-sized clothing; he was looking for a gift for his fiancée. I named the three that did out of hundreds in the mall and told him the size range for each. "That's not going to help," he said, "she's a size 32." He was shocked when I replied, "So am I!" (Fooled him, too!) This fellow confided that his fiancée—a woman with a loving man in her life and enough strength and savvy to support herself with a home-based business—seldom left her home because she felt she had nothing decent to wear. Because I've been sewing for more than 30 years, and even though I've worn every size from a 12 to a 32, I have never experienced that kind of social isolation. I have never hesitated to live my life fully because I had nothing to wear.

These incidents made me realize that I knew how to do something that many women do not. I know how to make comfortable clothes that enhance my appearance, are suitable for the occasion, and improve my self-esteem to the point that not only is my size not an issue, but also sometimes it isn't noticed at all.

If you are among the 1 in 15 women in this country who sew— and that's at least 4½-million plus-sized sewers—you can have any garment you want: any size, style, fabric, color, and designer name with comfortable and flattering fit. You no longer have to make do with the kind of ugly, ill-fitting, bulletproof-polyester circus costumes sold in many plus-sized shops and catalogs.

You only need basic sewing skills to use this book. If you haven't sewn for a while, brush up on your skills, get your machine tuned and lubed, and check out the chapter on tools so that you'll have what you really need. Please give yourself permission to make mistakes; we all do, and that's how we learn.

Even if you do not yet sew, the information on design, fabric, and fitting will make you a better-informed consumer of ready-to-wear. You can also use the appendix to hire a dressmaker to harvest the benefits of custom clothing without actually doing the work.

A NOTE ON NOMENCLATURE

I have used a variety of expressions to describe plus sizes, all of which fall short of semantic success. "Plus sized" begs the question "Plus what size?" Are thin and average women "minus sized?" The expression "full figured" sounds as if you must be voluptuously busty to qualify. "Women's" denotes all adult females, and I wouldn't call small or average women "little girls." "Queen sized" is simply silly. "Super sized" sounds like fast food. "Large" or "big" are fairly neutral and merely descriptive. Although "fat" is no more than a physical attribute, like eye color, many readers initially feel uncomfortable about calling themselves fat. One pithy nugget frequently expressed by size acceptance advocates, with tongue firmly in cheek, is "'Fat' is not a four-letter word; 'thin' is." A rose by any other name would smell as sweet.

sewing is
the solution

1

The average clothing size worn by women in this country is a size 14. If you wear any size larger than a 14, you are plus sized, and you're in great company. Nearly half of all women in the United States are plus sized, too! Plus-sized women come in all ages, in all sizes of large, and in a wide range of income levels and occupations, from socialite to factory worker, business executive to suburban homemaker. Most large women lead very busy, full, and ordinary lives. We need clothes for work, play, and special occasions just like our skinny sisters.

Artists have always celebrated the beauty and strength of big women. Visit an art museum or check out art books from your public library to look for artwork depicting plus-sized women. To get design ideas, note what styles of clothes are worn by the plus-sized subjects. When you look at nudes, notice how often artists choose Rubenesque models over tall and thin ones. Look at the body shapes of the women portrayed in the art and find at least one that looks like your body.

■ YOU ARE WHAT YOU WEAR

Many women of all sizes are unhappy with their bodies. We live in a culture in which size prejudice is the last socially acceptable form of bigotry. If you are plus sized, you may encounter prejudice every time you read your morning paper or whenever you do not see positive portrayals of large women in magazine ads and articles. You may go to work and wonder if an equally qualified coworker received the promotion you were hoping for because she is thinner than you are. If you go shopping in the evening, you may find that it's hard to find plus-sized clothes that fit you well in the styles that you want to wear and of the quality you want to invest in. It's no wonder that being big can get you down.

Because of size prejudice, your self-esteem may be low, and that means you may not be dressing very well. Have you put off making new clothes that would fit you as you are right now? Sometimes women of all sizes don't feel they deserve new things unless they first lose weight. Do you have a closet full of garments that are too tight, uncomfortable, embarrassing, and out-of-style? To add to the low-self-esteem factor, do you avoid social or career opportunities because "you have nothing to wear?" Unfortunately, if you don't value yourself very highly because of your size, the people around you may feel the same way.

The manner in which people of all sizes dress and groom themselves sends information to others around them about what kind of work or play they do, how they feel about themselves, and what their status and income level might be. If you are not dressing and grooming yourself well, you may be sending negative signals that reinforce the size stereotypes others may hold instead of positive signals that prove how wonderful you really are.

Instead of succumbing to low self-esteem, love yourself exactly as you are, put the current craze for thinness in its proper place, and live in the here and now. If you don't confuse thinness with morality and if you can put weight prejudice in its proper perspective, then you are ready to live life fully and actively. But no one can do this—legally anyway—by tearing around naked. We need clothes to wear.

You need to make choices about your wardrobe. You can leave your home as little as possible; you can wear your old clothes, even though they are too tight, uncomfortable,

Women lead such busy lives. It's so easy to put off sewing for ourselves because we are fulfilling everyone else's needs: The house needs cleaning, the boss wants you to work overtime, the kids need cupcakes baked for a school party, so who has time to sew? Here are a few things you can do to help make the time.

• When you visit a sewing store, buy everything you need to complete your project at the same time. For example, if you buy fabric, also select a pattern, thread, buttons or zipper, and trim to complete the garment.

• Keep a supply of frequently used notions on hand, such as elastic, stay tape, machine needles, and shoulder pads.

• Cut several projects out all at once on a weekend to save time setting up and cleaning up your cutting area.

• Spend 30 to 60 minutes a day sewing; in a week or two, you'll have a new outfit!

• Set up your sewing machine in your family room so you can interact with family members while sewing.

• Keep a small TV or radio near your sewing machine so you can lis-ten to music or watch the evening news while you sew.

• Take a portable phone to your sewing area so you don't have to jump up and answer calls; chat with friends and sew at the same time.

• Ask your family members to pitch in and help with housework, so that you have time to sew the clothes you need.

• Remind yourself and explain to your family and friends that for plus-sized women, sewing isn't merely an enjoyable hobby, it's a ticket to self-esteem.

unflattering, and out-of-style; or you can buy ready-to-wear that may not be the design, color, or quality you want and that probably doesn't fit well, either. On the other hand, if you're a plus-sized sewer, you can sew exactly what you want and need. Before we explore sewing as the solution to our clothing needs, it helps to understand the nature of the problems we often have with our clothes.

■ WHY YOU CAN'T FIND CLOTHES THAT FIT

Have you ever gone shopping, tried on dozens of outfits, but couldn't find anything that fit right? Ever wonder why? One big reason is that most designers and clothing manufacturers have never learned how to make clothes fit average women, much less plus-sized women!

Designers' deficiency

Many designers start their careers by attending a design school, and most of these schools teach garment design, patternmaking, draping, and fitting on small, standardized, commercial dress forms, usually a size 8. Standardized dress forms hold still for long periods of time without squirming or whining, and they won't sue you if you jab them with pins, but otherwise they aren't of much use. The forms are idealized in shape, with no figure variations whatsoever. Unlike the rest of us, they do not have dowager's humps, crooked hips, large bellies, love handles, DD busts, or any of the other figure variations common to all normal women of any size.

One famous New York designer admitted to a national talk show host how much she learned when her clothes were made for her personal friends: her friends' torso lengths were much shorter than those of her commercial dress forms and runway models. The only live models designers use are fit models, selected specifically because their measurements match a particular marketing profile. Designers typically have little or no training or experience in fitting average people. Many well-known designers admit that they have no idea how to design for large women, and that's probably true.

Manufacturers' mix-up

If you stop at your local minimart on the way home from work for ice cream, you could buy a pint, which is a precise measurement, or a scoop, which is not. You know that one clerk's scoop varies from another's, and the size of a scoop varies from shop to shop. However, whatever method of measure you choose, it's still ice cream.

Likewise, sizing is just a numbering system that allows clothing manufacturers and pattern companies to sell you their products in a way that enables you to select what you need. It helps to understand that some of these sizes are like pints and some of them are like scoops. You can't just look at a garment and guess whether the size number refers to a certain precise measurement, like a pint, or if it refers to some range of quantities, like a scoop. Whether you shop or sew, this is why you can wear such a wide and confusing range of sizes.

PATTERN COMPANY SIZES The major pattern companies use a certain set of measurements to draft their patterns in different sizes. These sets of measurements are called "standardized sizing." Current U.S. sizing specifications are based on measurements of young women who had just been discharged from the military after WWII. In this early study, researchers measured so few women over 200 pounds that they regarded the measurement data for larger sizes as statistically unimportant. They assumed one height for all women's sizes and added 2 in. to the bust and hips for each size increase, "as commonly practiced by the trade." So larger sizing was based on mathematical extrapolation, not on actual data from large-sized women.

In the late 1960s these numbers were modified slightly. These measurement specifications went up to a size 52, with bust, waist, and hip measurements of 56–51½–57 respectively, and a weight of 277 pounds. Even though this sizing information is now 30 years old, it is used consistently from one pattern company to another. That's why you can trust one pattern company's size 18 pants to fit about the same as another's.

READY-TO-WEAR SIZES Ready-to-wear manufacturers, on the other hand, can voluntarily comply with standards used by the major pattern

> **tip** *Instead of looking at the size label when shopping for ready-to-wear, take a tape measure with you. Check the circumferences of a garment and compare them to your own measurements. If the garment is bigger than you are, try it on.*

companies, or they can adopt any set of sizing standards they choose to attract a targeted market for their clothing. The numbers used to manufacture Lycra tank dresses for teenagers, for example, can differ from those used to make careerwear for mature women.

One reason that clothing manufacturers don't use the same sizing as the pattern companies is because of the successful sales trick called "vanity sizing." The ready-to-wear industry uses size labels as a marketing ploy to boost sales. They discovered that when two garments with similar fabric and construction compete for a consumer's dollars, that consumer will always buy the one with the smallest size number on it.

Sizing in ready-to-wear has become so inconsistent that some women can wear clothing in a range of four sizes. My custom clothing customers consistently buy garments at least two full sizes smaller than their pattern size. When a mature female relative of mine finally allowed me to make her a suit, I took her measurements and told her, "You're a size 24 on top and a 22 on the bottom." "What!" she sputtered, "That can't be right—I've worn a size 12 all my life!" And indeed she had, thanks to vanity sizing.

Even the vanity of individual designers impacts sizing. My dentist told me that his cousin works for a very famous New York designer who doesn't look fat but is a big gal, noticeably more so than her runway models. The largest size her firm makes has always been a 14, but the sizing standards the firm uses to manufacture her size 14 vary from year to year

as her weight cycles up and down, which drives consumers and retailers balmy but at least allows her to wear her own designs.

To add to the sizing confusion, many clothing manufacturers use CAD (computer-aided design) programs to skip the expense of making a sample garment for fitting on a dress form or fit model. With the hardware and software available, designers can produce photographically realistic printouts that actually display more detail than photos: They show a fabric's colors, patterns, drape, and texture. A model can be digitally photographed in an off-white outfit, a fabric image can be scanned and applied to the garment, and a catalog can be printed using that image. Then the clothes can be manufactured and sold to unsuspecting consumers—all without the actual garments ever having been worn by a human being.

When we go shopping and try on a dozen pairs of pants before we find one that fits, it's easy to think that something is wrong with our bodies. In fact, something is wrong with the pants. Remember that there is absolutely nothing wrong with your body; ready-to-wear may not meet your clothing needs. People should not fit clothes, clothes should fit people!

■ GOOD FIT MAKES YOU FEEL GREAT!

When you make your own clothes, they only come in one size, and that's the right size to fit your body. If you sew, size numbers are no longer a badge of virtue; they are just a numbering system. Moreover, clothes that properly fit your unique body enhance your appearance and self-esteem. They allow the beauty of the

learn that they have come to this conclusion because some styles in standardized sizes do not fit their figure variations. A large-busted woman, for example, may be convinced that she would not look good in a strapless evening gown because she has never seen herself in one that was correctly adjusted to fit her cup size. Likewise, a short-waisted woman may avoid dresses with waistline seams because she has never worn one that was adjusted for her waist length. When clothes fit right, you can comfortably and confidently wear a much wider variety of styles.

■ SEWING: THE SMART AND SATISFYING SOLUTION

Plus-sized sewers are so lucky! Instead of wasting time and money on shopping for clothes, you can sew any garment you want. Think of how much time you spend on shopping trips—three or four hours every weekend or so? In that time, you could cut and sew a well-fitting top, skirt, or pair of pants in your choice of fabric, style, and color for a fraction of the ready-to-wear price. If you sew your own clothes, you can express your taste, creativity, personality, and status. You can play along with fashion fads or ignore them completely by sewing classic, ethnic, or historic designs. If you enjoy shopping, don't worry! Even if you make nearly all your things, you'll still need to shop for shoes, accessories, and, of course, fabric!

Sewing even improves your health by reducing stress. A study published in a medical journal compared sewing to other activities requiring similar hand-eye coordination. The

> **tip** *If you are sensitive to size numbers, pretend you are in a foreign country that uses a different numbering system. If you were shopping in Europe and a fabulous suit fit you well, would you feel bothered that it was a size 42 instead of your usual size 16?*

garment's design and your personal beauty to shine without distraction.

Clothes that fit right are also more comfortable to wear. They give you room to walk, to sit down comfortably, and to stretch and bend over without constriction or embarrassing gaping. Clothes that fit well also last longer because there is less stress on the fabric and the seams than in clothes that are too tight.

In my custom clothing business, I often meet women who are convinced that they can't wear certain styles. After listening to them, I

researchers measured heart rate, blood pressure, and perspiration, all of which are common indicators of stress. Sewers, even beginners, showed the greatest rate of relaxation!

■ FASHION FIGURES FOR PLUS SIZES

Before you sew, take a quick look in the mirror to identify your basic body shape (compare it to the drawings below). Pear-shaped women are bigger below the waist than above the waist. Apple-shaped women are larger through the bust and midriff than they are in the hips. Potatoes are round all over and may have little or no waist definition. Super-sized women are usually big potatoes. There are also large women whose figures are well proportioned, with well-defined waists and fairly flat tummies that parallel the thin ideal; they are usually very tall and big-boned. I call them Madam Peanuts, in keeping with the richness of Mother Earth/fecund fruit and vegetable theme.

Look at the plus-sized fashion figures for apple, pear, potato, and Madam Peanut body

tip *Take copies of your fashion figure with you to the sewing store. Instead of looking at the fashion illustration or photo on the pattern, sketch out the design over your fashion figure so you can get a feel for how it will look on you.*

shapes, and select the one that looks most like you. Trace or copy the figure (see larger figures for tracing in Appendix A on p. 140). Then sketch out design ideas that you see on small figures in fashion magazines and pattern books to get a feel for what the design would look like on your body.

Use colored pencils or felt pens to experiment with combinations of color and surface features. You don't need any artistic skill or training to do this! Remember how much fun coloring books used to be? You don't even have to stay within the lines—just play and have fun!

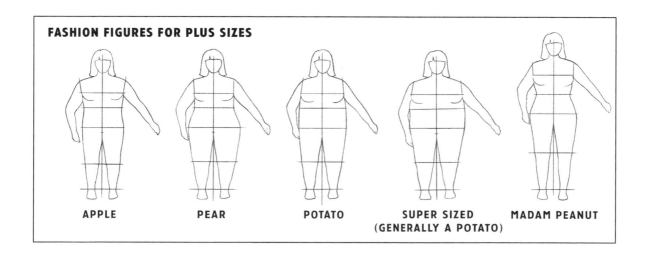

FASHION FIGURES FOR PLUS SIZES

APPLE   PEAR   POTATO   SUPER SIZED (GENERALLY A POTATO)   MADAM PEANUT

let's give them something to look at!

■ ■ 2 ■

The goal of all plus-sized design is to emphasize your positive attributes and modify or distract from those you feel are less desirable. The key here is that you and only you get to decide what you like or don't like. You may wish to enhance your face, hands, bodacious bustline, shapely legs, and so on. Or you may wish to deemphasize your bodacious bustline, belly, or upper arms.

Comfort levels vary from woman to woman. Someone with a large backside, for example, may wish to call attention to it with bows, fanny wraps, peplums, and other design features, while another woman might want to distract from it by decorating other parts of a garment to draw the eye away from that area.

However you feel about your body, you can make design decisions with style and creativity. In this chapter, you will learn what I affectionately call the "Let's Give Them Something to Look At" school of design. Our size attracts attention, so let's make the most of it!

■ WHAT TO EXPECT WHEN YOU SEW YOUR OWN CLOTHES

Don't expect that clothes can make you look thin. That's like saying that a red hat will make your blonde hair look red. Most wardrobe experts admit that dressing tips will appear to take off about 5 pounds at most.

If you are large, people are automatically going to look at you and notice you more than they do thin and average-sized women. We take up more space and naturally catch attention more readily. Many women go to great lengths to get noticed—all a big woman needs to do is walk in the room! If you work in sales or marketing, think what an advantage it is to be the one salesperson your potential client is bound to remember! We're hard to forget.

Because our visual presence is stronger, the signals we send with our choice of clothes and grooming is also relatively stronger. We need to take special care to select designs that send the right signals for our needs.

I don't believe in proscriptive dressing, nor am I going to dictate a catalog of completed garment designs guaranteed to make large

---

THE REAL QUEEN SIZE

Sir Hardie Amies has been dresser to Britain's Queen Elizabeth for more than 45 years. I often read criticisms of the Queen's garments from fashion people, but you know, her things are beautifully made, they fit her perfectly, and she is always dressed properly for the occasion—how many of us can say that? Her dressmaker advocates "Three Great Rules of Dress" that we would all do well to follow.

1. Clothes should not be too tight. Everyone looks best in clothes that skim the body and do not cling. Tight clothes look cheap and shout insecurity: The wearer either doesn't know her real shape or isn't happy with it. Too-tight clothes also form hori-zontal stress lines and wrinkles that can make anyone look wider. I have a magazine photo of a very famous and beautiful supermodel in a sheath that is so tight that the horizontal stress lines from bust to lower hips make her look like a bratwurst, even though she's built like a Slim Jim.

2. Clothes should fit the occasion. Don't try too hard or you may be overwhelmed by a design. There was a time when "noticing one's things" was an insult because if you stood out in a crowd, you weren't properly dressed for the occasion. This is why it's especially important to conform to whatever dress code is appropriate for your workplace. In Chris Browne's comic strip *Hagar the Horrible*, one morning the Viking Hagar is putting on his leather armor to get ready to go to work, and his wife Helga complains, "That outfit is so drab! Why don't you wear something eye-catching?" Hagar wearily replies, "Actually, when I'm going into battle, I kind of like to blend in." Isn't your workplace a battlefield, too?

3. Keep it simple. Fine fabric and construction show themselves off. Too many bells and whistles make a design look like a costume and can detract from the beauty of the woman within. As Sir Amies put it, "I have to ask myself, can this fancy idea work on a 50-in. bust?" He also noted, "The best way to judge a couturier is to select his ten fattest customers and see what he's done for them."

women look wonderful. There are too many variations in body shape, size, personal taste, comfort levels, fit preferences, and fashion trends to do so. However, if you understand the basic components of design, you can use these tools to select fabric colors and commercial patterns to enhance your appearance as only you desire.

■ THE COMPONENTS OF DESIGN

As a sewer, you have complete control of all the basic components of design. Just as a carpenter needs to know the difference between a jigsaw and a miter saw, plus-sized sewers need to understand the tools we use when we select styles to sew. Whether you know it or not, every time you get up in the morning and pull a navy skirt, white blouse, and red, white, and blue scarf out of your closet, you are designing. As a sewer, you get to select every component of design that suits you best.

Proportion

When we see an outfit in the mirror, on someone else, or in a pattern catalog, our eye automatically compares the smaller part of the outfit with the larger one. This comparison is called *proportion*. When the parts of an outfit are divided equally, the garment seems shorter and wider. A good example of even proportions is a Chanel-style suit, with a hip-length jacket and knee-length skirt. Uneven proportions keep the eye moving and give it interesting things to look at.

If you want to look taller and slimmer, avoid designs that chop you in half visually. Instead select styles with proportions of two-thirds to one-third, such as a fingertip-length jacket over a short skirt or a knee-length tunic over pants. Proportions of one-third to two-thirds are also pleasing, such as an Empire-waisted dress or a waist-length jacket with a long flared skirt (see the drawings on p. 14).

Width above and/or below an area makes that area seem smaller. For example, a flared skirt can make hips look less wide and shoulder pads with extended shoulders make the lower torso look narrower by comparison.

Note that the proportions of a garment sketched as a standard fashion figure or photographed on a thin model appear to change when that garment is worn by a plus-sized woman. That evenly proportioned Chanel-style suit, for example, looks fine on a thin model, but it looks boxy and awkward when drawn on a plus-sized woman (see the drawings on p. 14). This is also why many large women look as if they have short necks; even though their necks may not be shorter than average, they are wider than average, which makes them look shorter by comparison. No wonder many of us look better in any collar or neckline style that does not emphasize width across the neck (see the left drawings on p. 15).

Line

All the details that make up a design, such as seamlines, closure lines, trim lines, hemlines,

WORKING WITH PROPORTIONS

Proportions can be used to your advantage. Choose uneven proportions for a more flattering look.

Shoulder pads

This long jacket and short skirt combination is a good example of $2/3$–$1/3$ proportions, which are very flattering on a Madam Peanut.

An alternative to $2/3$–$1/3$ proportions might be an upper-hip-length jacket and lower-calf-length flared skirt, which work as $1/3$–$2/3$ proportions. The shoulder pads and flared skirt bring definition to an apple shape.

A Chanel-style suit looks fine on a standard fashion figure.

Put a Chanel-style suit on a plus-sized fashion figure, and the proportions don't work to her advantage. It looks boxy and awkward where uneven proportions would have looked great.

NECKLINE PROPORTION

If you are plus sized, your neck is as long as anyone else's. However, it can appear to be shorter because of the proportion of length to width. Horizontal design lines can emphasize that.

Standard fashion figure

Plus-sized fashion figure

and all other linear features, are called style lines. When you look at the black-and-white drawing of a garment on the back of a pattern envelope, all the lines you see are style lines.

VERTICAL LINES Vertical lines are a big woman's best friend. They draw the eye up and down and make the figure look taller and slimmer (see the drawings at right). Some examples are vertical closures, princess lines (especially those that meet the shoulder seam), pleats and softly draped gathers on pants and skirts, vertical contrast bands, vertically placed trim, vertical darts, vertical tucks, front keyhole necklines, and skirts with multiple gores.

HORIZONTAL LINES Horizontal lines cause the eye to pause as it looks you over, so they give the impression of width. You can place horizontal

VERTICAL DESIGN LINES

Design lines are all the details that you see on the black-and-white drawings on the back of your pattern envelope. Use them to emphasize what you love about your shape.

APPLE
Vertical design lines draw the eye up and down and make you look taller and slimmer. They are provided here by seams, flaps, contrast bands or trim, pleats, and buttons.

POTATO
On this potato shape, vertical design lines are given a softer look with a gored skirt with vertical draping, vertical gathers and darts on the blouse, and a long Chelsea collar. These strong elements overpower the horizontal waistband.

HORIZONTAL DESIGN LINES

Horizontal design lines make your eye pause, so put them where you want emphasis to balance out another feature or to draw attention to one.

Waist definition can take a variety of forms. A peplum with a back casing and tie will draw the eye to the waist.

Flaps, pockets, and epaulettes are all horizontal details that can be used to your advantage.

Layered or contrasting hemlines can add both color and horizontal lines at the waist, hem, or both.

lines in an outfit exactly where you want that width, for example, at the hipline to balance an apple-shaped figure, at the bust to balance a pear-shaped figure, at a flared hemline to make the waist of a potato look relatively smaller and to call attention to shapely calves, or at the waist if you're a well-proportioned Madam Peanut.

If you increase width above or below the waist with horizontal design lines, for example, your waist can look narrower in comparison. Peplums, blousing on bodices, gathers at the waist, and converging diagonal lines at the waist help create the illusion of narrowness. Jackets worn open to reveal a few inches of waistband are a slenderizing illusion, as are tucks, half

belts, or elastic casings that nip in at the waist. You can also try contoured facings instead of waistbands or shaped hip yokes on skirts and pants to reduce the number of widening horizontal lines at the waist and to lengthen the torso visually (see the drawings above).

Some other examples of horizontal design lines are shoulder and hip yokes; horizontal contrast bands; all horizontal seams and hems; pockets, welts, or flaps placed horizontally; square and bateau necklines; wing and Pilgrim collars; the straight upper edge of a bustier; horizontal shirring; horizontal tucks; cuffs on sleeves and trousers; and epaulettes and stiffened bows placed horizontally.

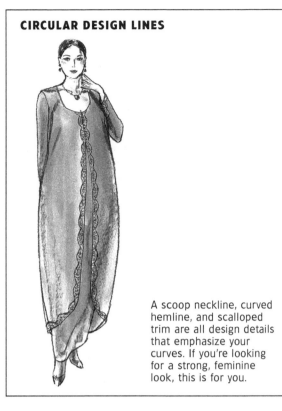

A scoop neckline, curved hemline, and scalloped trim are all design details that emphasize your curves. If you're looking for a strong, feminine look, this is for you.

Diagonal lines are another great look for plus-sized women. They are dynamic, slenderizing, and attractive. Here the diagonal hem, neckline, and drape create a great evening look.

CURVED LINES The curved lines in a garment are feminine, strong, and swingy. They also harmonize with the lines of our curvy bodies. If you don't like the roundness of your body, don't use curved lines. If you do, celebrate your fullness by selecting curved design lines in your clothes (see the drawing at left). Some examples are ruffles and flounces; jewel, scoop, U-shaped, and sweetheart necklines; Peter Pan, Bertha, band, and shawl collars; petal, bell, puffed, melon, Juliet, and leg 'o mutton sleeves; princess seams that end at the armscye; curved yokes and contrast bands; feather trim; cowl drapes; cocoon wraps; circular pockets and appliqués; curved welts for pockets and bound buttonholes; curved seaming and color blocking; circle skirts; and scallops or scalloped trim.

DIAGONAL LINES Diagonal lines in a garment's design are a big woman's second best friend. They are dynamic, slenderizing, and aesthetically pleasing (see the drawing at left). Some examples of diagonal design lines are diagonal seams and color blocking; diagonally placed gathers, pleats, shirring, or draping; sailor, spread, Chelsea, and notched collars; peaked or notched lapels; asymmetrical, surplice, halter, and V-necklines; petal sleeves; diagonally placed closures; handkerchief and asymmetrical hemlines; diagonally placed patch pockets, welts, and flaps; yokes with diagonal lines; French cuffs; tabs and belts with triangular-shaped ends; raglan-sleeve seamlines; trapeze- or wedge-shaped garments; kangaroo pockets; crossed or X-shaped straps on evening gowns; lacing; and soft, draped bows.

■ ANALYZING PROPORTION AND LINE IN PATTERN DESIGNS

Many plus-sized patterns currently available are extremely simple, with a loose and boxy fit. A plain princess-lined chemise, for example, doesn't give the eye much of anything interesting to focus on and only covers the body underneath. There is nothing else but the body shape for a viewer to look at.

You may wish to add a little more linear interest to a plain garment, as shown in the drawings on the facing page. For example, you could add pockets, trim, or piping to a plain, boxy cardigan jacket at selected seams and openings. Many designer patterns have complicated and interesting design lines. As you'll read later, you can wear these designs also, regardless of the pattern's size range.

Look for two-piece sleeves on jackets for more interesting vertical lines and better fit. Instead of flat-front pants (do you really have a flat front?), choose a style with vertical draping from pleats or gathers and a front fly to visually break up that great expanse across your hips and belly. This is what I mean when I refer to the "Let's Give Them Something to Look At" school of design.

Fabric as a design element

Once you have selected the design features you want in a pattern, you can start thinking about fabric, which I'll cover more later. For now, let's look only at the visual elements of fabric that contribute to a garment's total design.

COLOR Lighter and brighter colors seem to make an object look larger, while darker and duller colors tend to make the object look relatively smaller. Also, warm colors like red, orange, and yellow are perceived as advancing and give the illusion of weight, while cool colors like blue, green, and violet are experienced by viewers as receding and make objects look smaller.

Think of your body's basic shape and the proportions of your outfit. How will the colors you choose affect how a design looks on your body shape? Will they help balance the parts of the design or will the colors harmonize with and emphasize your body shape? When you're conscious of the way color functions as a design tool, you can select the results you really prefer (see the drawings on p. 20).

TEXTURE Next, consider the fabric's surface features. What is the fabric's texture? Shiny surfaces seem to make a surface look larger, while matte surfaces seem to make an object look smaller (see the drawings on p. 21). Rough or textured fabrics, such as corduroy, fuzzy

> **tip** *The next time you flip through a pattern book, before you think about which size to choose (I'll cover that later), just look at the line drawing on the back of the pattern instead of the idealized sketch or photo on the front. Analyze what kinds of lines there are, be they vertical, horizontal, circular, or diagonal, and ask yourself if that type of line and placement will enhance your figure.*

ANALYZING A PATTERN DESIGN

Learn to look at patterns with an eye to how the design lines will work for you and enhance your figure.

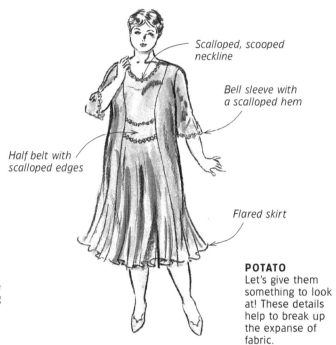

Scalloped, scooped neckline

Bell sleeve with a scalloped hem

Half belt with scalloped edges

Flared skirt

POTATO
Many plus-sized patterns tend to be boring with nothing to look at. All the viewer sees is the body shape.

POTATO
Let's give them something to look at! These details help to break up the expanse of fabric.

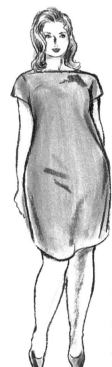

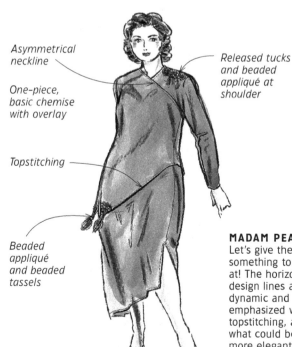

Asymmetrical neckline

One-piece, basic chemise with overlay

Topstitching

Released tucks and beaded appliqué at shoulder

Beaded appliqué and beaded tassels

MADAM PEANUT
Here's another case of nothing to look at. This plain chemise leaves the viewer with little to look at but a block of color.

MADAM PEANUT
Let's give them something to look at! The horizontal design lines are dynamic and emphasized with topstitching, and what could be more elegant than beading at the hip and shoulder?

WORKING WITH COLOR

Color is another element that you can use to your advantage.

PEAR
You can use color for balance. Lighter colors make objects look larger than darker colors. A light top with a dark bottom balances a pear-shaped figure.

APPLE
Here's another example of using light and dark colors for balance. A dark top with a light skirt balances an apple-shaped figure.

SUPER-SIZED POTATO
Cool colors like blue, green, and violet tend to recede, while warm colors like red, orange, and yellow come forward. A cool top and warm bottom make the torso look smaller and balances the large tunic with the small pants.

SUPER-SIZED POTATO
A warm top with a cool bottom looks unbalanced and makes the tunic look too big.

WORKING WITH TEXTURE

Fabrics come in every texture you can think of, and those textures are an important part of design. Shiny surfaces can look larger, while matte surfaces have the opposite effect.

APPLE
A velvet tunic has a luxurious matte texture, while the satin contrast bands and frogs add vertical design lines. The bulk of the textured top is balanced by the shiny satin pants.

PEAR
To balance a pear, you can draw the eye with a shiny satin top, and balance it with a tweedy textured skirt or pants.

SUPER-SIZED POTATO
The smaller, textured top balances the larger skirt. The top has sheer lace sleeves, lace over satin cups, and scalloped lace trim, while the skirt is a matte taffeta A-line.

woolens, fleece, velvet, chenille, lace, bouclé, heavy tweed, or quilted fabrics, increase apparent size, but they also distract from the shape of the body underneath. The same is true for stiff and crisp fabrics such as duchesse satin, taffeta, canvas, poplin, or organza. If you're pear-shaped, you could wear a satin blouse with a tweed skirt, or if you are an apple, you could wear a velvet tunic over satin pants to achieve balance. For a potato or Madam Peanut shape, a wedding dress with a lace-covered Empire bodice and a matte taffeta skirt would distract from the shape of the torso underneath and add apparent weight to the bustline, where many of us would want it.

PATTERN Woven or printed patterns on fabrics also contribute to a garment's overall design. Prints with light, bright colors and sharply

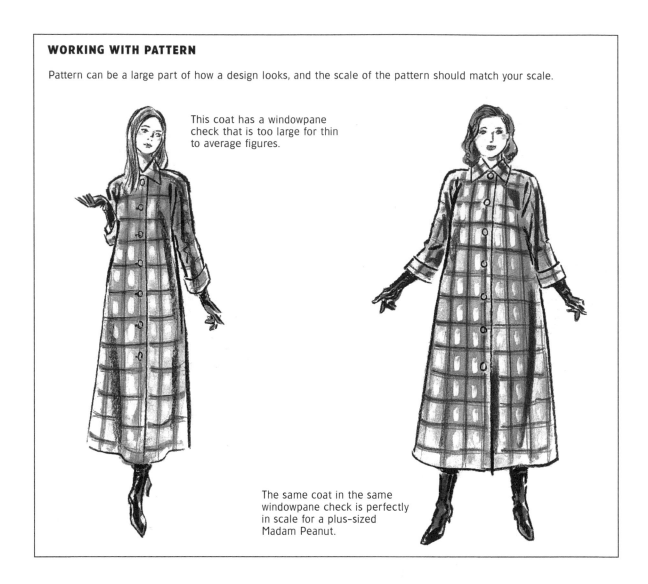

WORKING WITH PATTERN

Pattern can be a large part of how a design looks, and the scale of the pattern should match your scale.

This coat has a windowpane check that is too large for thin to average figures.

The same coat in the same windowpane check is perfectly in scale for a plus-sized Madam Peanut.

defined motifs make garments look larger, while darker, muted, less focused, or fuzzier prints make objects look relatively smaller. Directional prints draw the eye across a garment, so they function just like design lines. Vertical patterns, such as stripes, wide wales in corduroy, or long-stemmed roses printed with flowers up and stems down are lengthening, while horizontal patterns like the crosswise rib in ottoman or crosswise stripes are widen-

ing. Prominent twill weaves, plaids, and stripes cut on the bias and diagonally placed printed patterns function as diagonal lines. Polka dots and swirly motifs work the same as curved design lines.

Also think about the scale of the patterns on a fabric. While a thin to average-sized woman might be overwhelmed by a widely spaced windowpane check on a coat, for example, a larger woman could carry it off because the pattern is in scale with her body size (see the drawings on the facing page). Unless you have very fine features, such as fine curly hair, small prints and motifs may get lost on you. Try larger and more widely spaced patterns to harmonize with your body size.

Special design concerns for plus-sized women

As a plus-sized woman, you may also have some unique physical needs that can affect what kind of garment designs work best for you. Body fat is an excellent insulator. Big people generally feel warm year-round, so we usually feel best in lightweight, breathable fabrics.

ACCESSORIES AS DESIGN ELEMENTS

Use the information on design line and fabric surface features to select scarves, jewelry, shoes, hose, and handbags to complete an outfit. For example, a long necklace or large pendant on a large chain creates an attractive vertical or diagonal line on a plain jewel-necked top. On the other hand, a choker necklace on a large neck creates a widening horizontal line, which makes the neck look relatively shorter. A scarf folded triangularly over one shoulder and knotted at the other shoulder makes an accentuating diagonal line across the upper torso and brings attention away from the body to the face. Hose and shoes in the same color and value as a skirt can change unattractive one-half to one-half proportions of a tucked-in blouse and knee-length skirt to more flattering one-third to two-thirds proportions.

If you sew basic, classic garments in fine fabrics that will last for many years, accessories are an easy, fun, and inexpensive way to update your wardrobe and play with fashion fads. If $5,000 chartreuse satin evening gowns embroidered all over with oriental floral motifs are in, treat yourself to ¼ yard of a similar fabric, hem the edges, and tuck the scarf into the neckline of your basic black suit for an instant renewal.

ACCESSORIES

PEAR
You can change unflattering ½–½ proportions to ⅓–⅔ just by selecting hose and shoes in the same color as the skirt.

Outfits with many layers, for example, may feel too warm for comfort, and thick layers may look bulky as well.

Friction from body parts rubbing together, for example at the inner thighs, can cause abrasion and eventually holes in some fabrics. Some seams may be stressed and may need reinforcement, particularly in pants.

The fat areas of our bodies are more movable and compressible than the muscular areas, so our choice of shapewear has a much greater effect on plus-sized design and fit than for harder-bodied women. When we sit, our bellies, fannies, and thighs spread more than thin people's do, and this spread affects comfort and fit for any garment from the waist down. For example, flat-front pants with a close fit through the crotch, like most jeans, may look and feel fine when you are standing but may pull uncomfortably along the crotch seam and side seam when you sit down. Pleated or gathered pants styles give you the room for spread that you may need.

For the same reason, short skirts that are straight or pegged will ride up on the thighs of a large body more than on a small body; the fabric pulls into horizontal folds when the backside and thighs spread when a wearer is seated. Many plus-sized women also find gluing their knees together to sit modestly in short skirts particularly tedious. Longer, looser skirts with a bit of flare at the hem may be more comfortable for plus-sized women to sit in. Of course, you can still wear those fashionable jeans or that short, sexy skirt if you want

to because when you are your own designer, you get to make all the choices!

■ ABOUT YOUR UNDERWEAR

If your self-esteem is low and you are just starting to sew for the body you really have, the underwear you own may not fit and function the way you need it to. To carry off a garment's design and not detract from it, you need appropriate underwear.

For a strapless evening or wedding gown or a low V-backed gown, for example, you need a boned, strapless, or strapless/backless bra. Clingy knits call for a smooth, seamless-cup bra. With activewear, forget the bones and underwires; you need a comfortable, breathable sports bra. Likewise for panties and body suits. Slips are like instant linings: They add opacity and smoothness to any garment and help prevent clothes from clinging to your body. You should have full and half-slips to wear with whatever lengths of skirts and dresses you own.

Making your own bras is an option, but most bras are heavily constructed and require difficult-to-find fabrics and fixtures. Panties in Lycra swimwear fabrics or power net are easy and fast to sew yourself. Treat yourself to a half-slip in prewashed silk charmeuse or China silk with gorgeous lace trim, and you'll never wear cold, slimy nylon tricot again!

Another possible solution to the underwear dilemma is to look up "Brassieres" in your Yellow Pages to find a local, old-fashioned corset shop (see Resources on p. 149). Most large towns and cities have at least one. The fitters who work in these shops are experts at determining your correct size and the best style for your shape, plus these shops specialize in hard-to-find styles and sizes. The inexperienced teenaged clerks at your local mall and the inadequate measuring instructions in catalogs won't help you much.

Once you know your correct size, you can order from catalogs, but beware that the undergarments from many budget sources are inaccurately sized, poorly fabricated, and badly constructed.

■ LISTEN TO YOUR COMPLIMENTS

The next time you receive a compliment, analyze what the viewer might have perceived as attractive: the color choices you made, the proportions, the design lines, or the surface features of the fabric? Your admirer probably won't know exactly why he or she liked the outfit on you, but if you get more compliments when you dress a certain way, you can figure out why and repeat that performance in other garments.

Also, pay attention to the way garments make you feel. Have you ever worn a "lucky" interview suit, a sexy peignoir, a uniform that made you feel authoritative, a sportswear outfit in happy colors, or an evening gown that made you feel elegant? Our clothes are our most immediate environment: They are where we live. How they make us feel is as important as how they make us look.

tools for plus-sized sewing

■ ■ 3 ■

All sewers need good quality equipment that is in good repair. There is nothing more frustrating than trying to cut cloth with dull shears, for example, and no bigger waste of time than waiting for an automatic shut-off iron to heat up each time you're ready to press a seam or fighting with a bobbin that jams constantly. In addition, plus-sized sewers have some special equipment needs. Take the time to evaluate your equipment, particularly if you haven't done much sewing for a while. Then you can replace or repair whatever doesn't work for you *before* you're in the middle of a project.

■ FURNITURE

Your sewing machine table should be sturdy and nonvibrating as well as a comfortable height. Larger sewing machine tables can hold both your conventional sewing machine and your serger as well as other equipment such as a cone thread stand, hand tools, and a cup of coffee.

Your cutting table also should be sturdy, and it should be wide enough to hold an unfolded width of fabric, long enough to lay out all the pieces for a single garment (or at least 6 ft. long so you can match patterns more easily as you lay out the pieces), and tall enough for you to keep your back straight while cutting. Which would you rather have: tired arms or a tired back?

The collapsible cardboard contraptions sold in sewing stores are inadequate in height, width, length, and sturdiness. Your dining room

table (with the pads on for protection against pin scratches) will do, and you can temporarily raise the height of any table by slipping books or large cans under the legs. A Ping-Pong table, a cleared kitchen counter, or a hollow door laid across a couple of two-drawer filing cabinets can work in a pinch. If you don't have a good cutting table, you can always crawl around on the floor if your knees can handle the beating. If they can't, ask family and friends for help with pinning and cutting.

If your mobility is restricted, you may need to lower your cutting table height. I spoke to a disabled, plus-sized dressmaker who cuts out garments on a large glass coffee table from her wheelchair, which works just fine for her.

Your sewing chair should be height adjustable. If you get tired or achy after hours of sewing or if you have trouble focusing on your work, try changing your chair height and the position of the back support occasionally to work a different set of muscles. A gas-lift secretarial chair on wheels with a well-padded, wide seat works great. Be sure that the seat base is made of durable plywood, not pressboard, which will eventually crumble and crack apart with use; lift up the paper covering on the underside of the seat to examine it. A flimsy folding chair or stool will not give you the height or back support you need.

Good lighting is crucial. You can't sew what you can't see. Natural and overhead lighting needs to be augmented with task lights, which are small, incandescent, fluorescent, or halogen lights on clips or swing arms, that allow you to direct light exactly where you need it. You may

> tip *If your tummy or the type of sewing table you are using prevents you from sitting close enough to your machine, you may get back or neck pain from leaning over to see your work, particularly if you wear bifocals. Try slipping two art gum erasers under the base of your machine in the back, so the throat plate and foot area are tilted down and so are easier to see. Having plenty of knee space underneath the sewing table also helps.*

CONSTRUCT A CUSTOM CUTTING TABLE

My wonderful gateleg cutting table was made by my handy husband. It's made of plywood and is on casters so I can move it easily. Collapsed, it measures 4 ft. wide by 18 in. deep by 41 in. tall. When it's open, the cutting surface measures 4 ft. by nearly 8 ft.! You can build one of these with easy-to-find materials and basic carpentry skills. When you finish your table, try using a tung oil finish instead of polyurethane since scratches from pins and scissors are inevitable. It's easy to touch up scratches with a dab of stain and finishing oil.

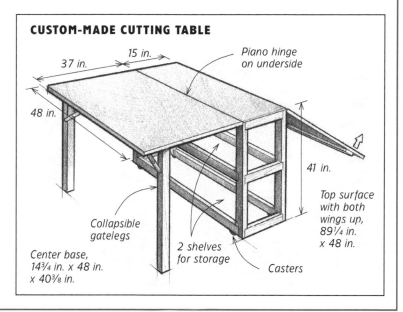

CUSTOM-MADE CUTTING TABLE

37 in.

15 in.

Piano hinge on underside

48 in.

41 in.

Top surface with both wings up, 89¼ in. x 48 in.

Collapsible gatelegs

Center base, 14¾ in. x 48 in. x 40⅜ in.

2 shelves for storage

Casters

---

need separate task lights for your machine, cutting area, and pressing area.

Mirrors are essential for plus-sized sewing. You can't fit yourself if you can't see yourself. You can mount an inexpensive full-length mirror on the back of a door to save wall space. Either sliding or bifold mirrored closet doors can replace standard doors and are easy to install. A large, inexpensive hand mirror works well to provide a back view for fittings.

■ SEWING MACHINES

There is almost no sewing technique that you cannot accomplish on a very basic, standard sewing machine. You don't need a fancy $3,000 model that cuts the thread and embroiders little ducks. Remember that you do the sewing, not the machine.

All you really need is a heavy-duty, mechanical or electronic model with a backstitch and a zigzag stitch that you can use to make respectable buttonholes. A used or refurbished model can be a better option than a cheaper, newer model—they don't always make them like they used to. A nice-looking automatic buttonhole and some basic utility stitches, such as a multiple zigzag stitch, blindstitch, blanket stitch, and straight stretch stitch, are very helpful.

Sergers are like microwave ovens. When you first get one, you think it can do everything. Eventually you learn that it is not wise to try to shove a turkey into a microwave, and with experience, you will learn which sewing techniques work best on a standard machine and which work best on a serger.

Sergers are wonderful for neat, fast seam allowance finishes; fast and stretchy seams for

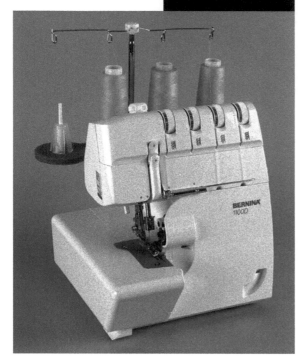

ing your vacation when you can live without them for a week. A good quality and well-maintained sewing machine for most home sewers can last 10 to 20 years.

Some helpful, basic machine accessories include a variety of machine needles, both regular point for woven fabrics and ball point for knits, in a range of sizes. You should routinely change your machine needle after every project or so to maintain good stitch quality. A collection of presser feet, such as straight and zigzag feet, with their accompanying straight and zigzag needle plates, and conventional and invisible zipper feet, are essential. If your machine did not come with these, most notions catalogs or your repair technician can provide them. You also need a very small and a medium flathead screwdriver for routine machine adjustments.

Keep plenty of bobbins on hand, stored in a plastic bobbin box, so you won't have to unwind and then rewind a bobbin to change thread colors. Note that some plastic bobbins wear out and need replacing occasionally. My machine uses a bobbin with a tiny metal spring on the underside, which sometimes comes poorly finished with a burr that catches the thread and jams the bobbin. Either file off the burr or replace the bobbin to solve that problem.

knits; and attractive rolled hems on apparel and household linens. A basic, mechanical 3/4-thread model with a rolled-hem capability will serve you well (see the photo above). Be sure to change the lower blade whenever it starts to cut poorly; silks and most synthetics dull the blade quickly. Keep an extra lower blade on hand to save time.

Keep your machines lubricated, if mechanical, and keep them clean. Always clean lint from around the bobbin case, feed dogs, needle, needle plate, and thread guides with a small stiff-bristled brush to maintain good performance. Have your machines professionally cleaned and checked once a year, perhaps dur-

■ MEASURING AND DRAFTING TOOLS

You can't fit your body if you don't know how big it is, and you can't adjust patterns to fit you better if you don't have the right drafting tools (see the photo on the facing page). Buy a

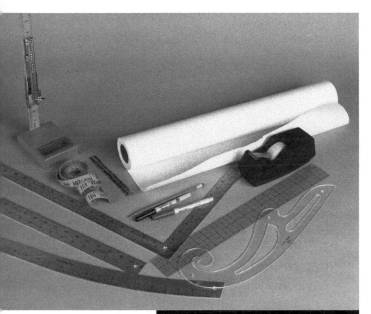

Pioneer women made do with pieces of string to measure for their family's clothing. Luckily, these helpers are easy to find at sewing and office supply stores. Clockwise from the bottom left: hip curve, yardstick, L-square, hem marker, 120-in. tape measure, sewing gauge, drafting paper, an assortment of pens and pencils, tape, gridded clear plastic ruler, and French curve.

flimsy to be accurate since the sliding marker will not stay where you put it.

You need several rulers, such as the clear plastic variety imprinted with ⅛-in. grids and slots at various distances from the edge, for fast and easy sizing adjustments. French curves or hip curves allow you to draw curved seamlines. An L-square or T-square from a hardware store or a sewing supply source will help you square off fabrics and establish pattern lines.

A hem marker is like a yardstick mounted on a base. The pin-through variety requires a helper to pin up hems; the chalk kind allows you to squeeze a handheld bulb to squirt a chalk line at whatever height you choose as you rotate in front of the marker. There is nothing that looks tackier on plus-sized women than an uneven hemline, unless the hem is meant to be asymmetrical.

Drafting paper is crisp, translucent, and inexpensive; it's available from office supply stores and comes 36 in. wide on a tube. It is good for drafting, copying, and adjusting patterns. Do not cut this with your sewing shears! The brightening chemicals in standard papers dull scissors very quickly.

An assortment of colored pencils or felt pens allows you to sketch out designs and mark pat-

120-in. tape measure, available at most sewing stores and through notions catalogs. Going around twice with a standard 60-in. tape measure just isn't accurate, particularly if any part of you is greater than 60 in. in circumference.

A yardstick is useful for drawing long, straight lines and for measuring hem lengths up from the floor. It should be heavy, shellacked hardwood or metal, not a flimsy freebie from the county fair.

A sewing gauge looks like a short ruler, with a movable plastic marker that rides in a slot in the middle. It is handy for measuring hem widths, button placement, pleat and tuck widths, and so on. If you can bend it, it's too

tip *If you don't yet have a hem marker, try this trick. Chalk a string heavily, thumbtack it across a door frame at your desired hem height, and rub your skirt up against the string to mark it.*

tern adjustments. Transparent tape, preferably in a heavy dispenser so you can pull off pieces one-handed, is essential for adjusting patterns.

■ CUTTING TOOLS

All your scissors and shears must match your handedness—lefties for lefties and righties for righties. The handles should be large enough to fit your hand and fingers comfortably. Some specialty scissors have small finger holes, which can be uncomfortable to use. Generally, bent-handled shears are more comfortable to hold than scissors. Larger and sharper scissors are less tiring for your hand than smaller, duller ones.

Specialty scissors include pinking shears, which you can use to finish seams and soften the look of interfacing edges. Some sewers like to grade convex-curved seams with pinking

shears since this automatically notches the seam allowance to reduce bulk. I've found that although pinking shears can be sharpened, they often seem duller after I have them sharpened than beforehand. Buy the best quality you can afford, so that they may not need sharpening for a long time.

Thread clips are about 4 in. long, are mounted with a spring, and are squeezed to clip threads or seams. Some of these have small finger holes but can be operated by just squeezing the blades. Pelican scissors, also called duckbill or appliqué scissors, may also have small finger holes, but their points are very small and sharp and they are excellent for grading seams and trimming appliqués.

Electric rotary-blade scissors can be a godsend if you have arthritic hands. They are quiet and do not vibrate like the old-fashioned kind with straight blades. Some electric scissors are rechargeable and some are self-sharpening. With mine, I do have trouble seeing exactly where I'm trying to cut, especially small, angled cutting lines, since the bulk of the device obscures my view of the cutting blade.

Manual rotary cutters are razor-sharp wheels on handles, which must be used with a protective plastic mat. Sewers either love them or hate them. They're great for cutting small pieces accurately; try using one against a ruler for straight lines. I find moving my mat around under garment pieces as I cut to be time-consuming; and while I only need one hand to cut with shears, with a rotary cutter I need both hands—one hand to hold the fabric and one to cut.

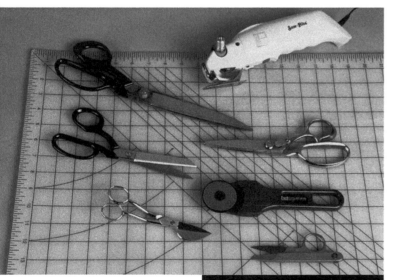

Select a variety of cutting tools that meet your physical and sewing needs best. From the top: electric rotary-blade scissors, large tailor's shears, pinking shears, bent-handled shears, rotary cutter, pelican scissors, and thread clips.

All cutting equipment must be kept sharp. Knife-edge shears are easy to sharpen at home with a whetstone. There is an electric scissors sharpener designed for home use, which works very well. Otherwise, most sewing stores offer sharpening services; plan to use them at least two to four times a year. Remember to use your sewing scissors only for fabric! Train your family never to use them for cutting paper or any other household use, or they will quickly become too dull to cut cloth.

■ MARKING TOOLS

You need a variety of marking tools to mark garment pieces for darts, tucks, pocket placement, and other construction details (see the photo below). You should have an assortment of colored tracing paper and a tracing wheel that makes a straight or dotted line. Tracing paper should wash and dry-clean out; check the package. The air-soluble kind smells terrible and frequently comes out before you have time to sew the garment. Use as light a shade as you can see or one that closely matches the fabric. Don't use tracing paper on sheer or fragile fabrics. Only use it on the inside of garments, never on the outside, since the marks are not always easy to remove.

Thread is used to mark garment pieces with tailor's tacks or thread tracing. Don't use bright, contrasting colors because some threads may crock, or bleed color onto fabric, or small fiber pieces from colored thread can stick to and discolor light fabrics. A better thread for marking is cotton basting thread, which is a heavy, glazed hand-sewing thread. The glaze helps prevent errant thread fibers from sticking to your fabric and makes hand sewing easier. Quilting thread is a good substitute. Silk thread is wonderful for all hand sewing, and it won't leave impressions when you press after removing the tacks or tracing. It's strong, doesn't shred, and creates little friction as you pull it through fabric, so it does not tangle as badly as poly or poly/cotton thread. Run all your hand-sewing threads over a piece of beeswax to strengthen and lubricate them and to reduce tangling.

Tailor's chalk is either the chalk type, which brushes off, or the wax type, which presses out. Use wax chalk only for woolens because the mark can leave a greasy stain on other fabrics. Sharpen these small bricks of chalk with a knife. A chalk wheel is a small container of

Choose a marking method that is appropriate for each fabric you sew. Some of the tools you need are, from left, threads for tailor's tacks or thread tracing, a creasing tool, a tracing wheel, beeswax, tailor's chalk, marking pens, and tracing paper.

loose chalk that is dispensed through a small serrated wheel; it makes a fine, sharp line and can be used with a ruler to make very straight lines.

Marking pencils can be air soluble, water soluble, graphite, or chalk based. A quilter's pencil uses a soft graphite, which is specially formulated to launder out. A soapstone pencil is a natural substance that makes a light-toned mark on firm fabrics and can be sharpened like a pencil. A creasing tool is plastic with a sharp edge, which can leave a temporary mark on firmly woven fabrics that can be pressed out. You need to replace your felt-pen markers fairly frequently. Always test your markers on a scrap of fabric to make sure that the marks are removable.

■ PRESSING TOOLS

Half of sewing is pressing, so you need an assortment of tools to do it right (see the photo on the facing page). Since you will sew and press for many hours at a time, do not use an automatic shut-off iron. It will drive you crazy when you have to wait for it to heat up every time you need to press. A Teflon soleplate or separate iron shoe will help prevent the buildup of resins and starches. Use an iron cleaner, available from sewing stores, in a well-ventilated area to keep your soleplate clean. Allow steam irons to heat up enough to produce steam; otherwise, they may merely drip.

Your ironing board needs to be height adjustable so you can iron comfortably while seated. It needs to be sturdy and not tippy, especially if you have little people or pets in the house. The flimsy foam pad that comes with an ironing board cover is inadequate. Replace it with layers of wool fabric or cotton padding, such as a piece of an old mattress pad. Generally, you need at least ½ in. of dense padding. Teflon-coated ironing board covers reflect too much heat and may cause bubbling when you fuse interfacings. Plain, sturdy cotton muslin or duck is best. Unless you sew your own cover, it will shrink too much when you wash it to fit back on the board, so you'll have to buy a new one.

You must have a variety of pressing aids. These will all last a lifetime. A press cloth protects fabrics from accidental scorching, shine, and press marks. Always use one when pressing the outside of a garment. A piece of light-colored cotton or linen with the edges pinked or serged or even an old, gauze burping diaper works fine.

tip *A spritz from a utility sprayer makes quick work of stubborn wrinkles on fabrics that do not water spot. It can set seams, make creases sharp, and remove water-soluble-pen marks.*

tip *A small, handheld steamer is helpful for steaming a completed garment on a hanger or dress form to encourage the fabric to drape gracefully. It also substitutes for a travel iron.*

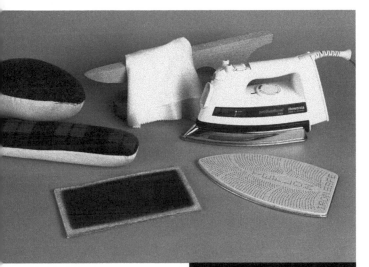

Many pressing tools reproduce the curves of your body, so you can shape fabric to conform to those curves as you press. Some pressing tools make pressing during construction easier and faster. From the left: tailor's ham, sleeve roll, point presser, press cloth, needle board, iron, Teflon soleplate.

tip *You can easily make a sleeve roll yourself. Just tightly roll up a large magazine like* W, *and use a couple of small strips of tape to hold the roll together. Cover the roll smoothly with a cotton flannel rectangle to go around the roll and make two circles to cover the ends of the roll; slipstitch the pieces in place. If desired, make a second cover that is removable so you can launder it. Cut a rectangle of muslin and sew it like a tight pillowcase; slip it over the flannel-covered roll. My sleeve roll is like a time capsule, with 30-year-old* Ladies' Home Journals *inside.*

A tailor's ham reproduces body curves. Use one on all darts, curved seams, collars, and cuffs. A collapsible sleeve board makes pressing sleeve seams open and ironing sleeves easier, but a sleeve roll can also be used to press seams open on fragile fabrics like satin, without producing unattractive ridge lines on the right side from the seam allowances.

A point presser is an odd-looking hard-wood contraption that can be used with or without pads to press open very small and hard-to-reach areas of a garment. A needle-board looks like a miniature bed of nails; it is essential for pressing velvet and other pile and fleece fabrics. The needles hold the pile up so the iron does not flatten it. A stiff-bristled clothes brush helps lift nap and removes thread and lint from your project and your own clothes.

■ HAND TOOLS

You do not need a room full of gadgets; you need only the basics (see the photo on p. 36). Start with a variety of hand-sewing needles in a range of sizes. I like milliner's needles because they are long and fast for running stitches, have a fine eye that is easy to pull through fabric, and are easy for my large hands to hold. Pins with large plastic heads, like quilter's pins, are easier for large hands to grasp, and the heads prevent wear and tear on the fingertips.

For hand sewing, thimbles for your middle finger prevent pain and injury. The leather ones are comfortable and do not cut thread as metal

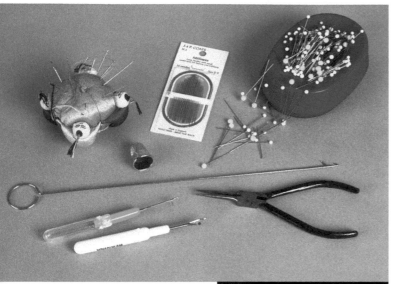

Nearly all handicrafts require hand tools. Sewers only need these few: pincushions, thimbles, hand-sewing needles, straight pins, a bodkin, seam rippers, and needle-nosed pliers.

tip *A note on clothes hangers: The standard, 16-in. wire hangers you get back with your dry cleaning are not wide enough to support your clothes and help them keep their shape without drooping and forming wrinkles while in your closet. You can find 18-in. jacket hangers and 19-in. men's coat hangers from dry-cleaning stores or store fixture sources (see Resources on p. 149). You may have to buy them in large quantities, so perhaps you could share or sell some to your plus-sized friends. Inexpensive, stretchy foam hanger pads are also available; they help prevent wire impressions from forming on your clothes and prevent garments from slipping off hangers onto your closet floor.*

thimbles can. Fingercots are a couple of inches long and look like the snipped-off tip of a latex glove; they are available at pharmacies (they're used for rectal exams—you had to ask) in several sizes. They both protect your needle-pushing finger and help grip the needle. Even an adhesive bandage will work in a pinch.

Seam rippers should be replaced when dull. I used the same seam ripper for more than 30 years until the handle broke in half. I found the new one was much sharper and worked much faster! Larger ones will fit your hand better. All sewers use these.

Have two pincushions, one for pins and one for needles, so that the thread tails from your needles won't become tangled in your pins. A bodkin or loop turner makes fast work of turning spaghetti straps and other fabric tubes.

Small, needle-nosed pliers are great for yanking the staples out of button cards and for grabbing all sorts of things. A tiny latch hook, often called a knit picker, is useful for burying the tails of hand- and machine-sewing threads inside a garment and for repairing snags. Keep a nail file handy to keep your nails smooth so that they don't snag fine fabrics.

■ DRESS FORMS FOR PLUS SIZES

You can cut your fitting time in half if you have a dress form that looks like you. All forms need a sturdy base and should be height adjustable or correspond correctly with your height.

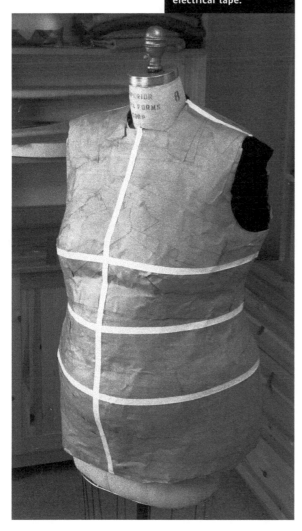

dress size 44 to 50, with maximum bust, waist, and hip measurements of 55–47–57. Another model goes up to a size 22, with maximum dimensions of 44–36–46.

The problem with home-sewing forms and their much more expensive commercial counterparts is that they are idealized and do not look like us. They do not have small or pendulous breasts, droopy or perky fannies, swaybacks, or any other figure variation. You can try padding a standard dress form to look and measure like you by attaching concentric circles of polyester batting to the form with tape, by using preformed foam pads designed specially for this purpose, or even by using bath towels. Pieces of black twill tape pinned to the form at bust, waist, hips, center front, center back, and style lines will help with the fitting process.

Commercial forms can be custom-made to match anyone's dimensions, but they can be quite expensive and cannot be adjusted if you change shape or size.

Homemade forms are a better option for plus-sized sewers. One system uses a custom-fit muslin cover filled with foam; it is available up to a size "large," or measurements of 50–44–51. Some sewers make a form by wrapping their plastic-covered torsos in plaster bandages from a medical supply source to make a body cast that is subsequently filled with insulation foam; the hardened foam becomes the form. This is a cold and sloppy process, it's hard to find the bandages, and the foam smells acrid, irritates the airways, and is also difficult to find. Try making the cheap and easy paper dress form on pp. 38–39.

The home-sewing dress forms available in sewing stores or catalogs have some advantages. They are easy to adjust vertically and horizontally within a range of sizes, have sturdy bases, and frequently come with chalk-type hem markers. However, they may not be big enough for you. One model goes up to a

MAKING A PERSONAL
PAPER-TAPE DRESS FORM

One cheap (costs less than $5), very easy, and completely non-toxic way to make your own dress form has been around since the 1930s. I learned it in 4-H more than 30 years ago. You will need a helper; "significant others" can be too easily distracted and may not take direction well, so recruit a sewing friend and make forms for each other.

For each form, you will need one 600-ft. roll of 2-in.-wide paper tape, the old-fashioned kind that looks like brown Kraft paper on one side and has wetable glue on the other (see Resources on p. 149 for a mail-order source). Do not use any other type of carton-sealing tape, including plastic tape or paper tape with nylon reinforcements.

Be forewarned that the layers of tape will dry as you work and will eventually feel rigid. If you are the least bit claustrophobic, you may feel panicky as the tape hardens. To make the form, follow these steps.

1. Start by wearing your usual underwear and a tight, form-fitting, jewel-necked T-shirt or turtleneck that comes down well over the widest part of your hips. It can be old, holey, or stained since you won't see it when the form is completed. Before you start, be sure to use the bathroom! You need to be able to stand for about two hours without a break.

2. Put a large sponge in a basin or sink of water, and use it to moisten strips of paper tape by running the strip of tape over the wet sponge. Cover the roll of tape with a towel as you tear off strips since drips will glue the layers of the roll together. Wrap the strips snugly, slightly overlapping them, around the figure over the T-shirt. Use shorter, diagonally placed strips to define the curves of the bust, neckline, and armscyes and longer strips to wrap the torso horizontally, mummy-style.

3. Wrap about three layers of tape evenly over the wrapee, with some extra layers around the neck, armscye, and lower edge for durability. At this point the wrapee is going to look like a large, walking, talking Baked Potato Woman, and you will both be giggling hysterically.

4. When you are finished wrapping, use a hair dryer to dry the tape thoroughly, or the form will lose its shape when you remove it.

Start by defining the finished edges of the form. The glue on the paper tape will stick to the T-shirt underneath.

This stage of taping is like mopping your kitchen floor. Try to remember where you've been and where you're going as you evenly build up three or four layers of tape.

5. When the form is quite rigid, use a sturdy pair of large shears to cut the form carefully up the center back, right through the T-shirt but hopefully not through the wrapee's underwear. Carefully pry open the form to allow the wrapee to escape. Then use more paper tape on the underside and the outer side of the form to seal the cut up the center back.

6. Once completely dry, you can hang the form on a hanger, set it on a table, make a T-shaped stand with three pieces of PVC pipe and a T-joint mounted in a Christmas tree stand, or try my favorite method: Just pop it over a skinny dress form. You can complete the form with spray paint or with a clean T-shirt or Lycra tube that you can pin into.

7. Style lines can be established with felt pen or black twill tape for fitting and patternmaking.

A paper-tape dress form is nontoxic, lightweight, firm, smooth, durable, and exactly reproduces the wrapee's posture and figure variations. Circumference measurements come out a little larger than the body's but that actually helps with the fitting process. If your size and shape changes, it's easy and inexpensive to make a new one.

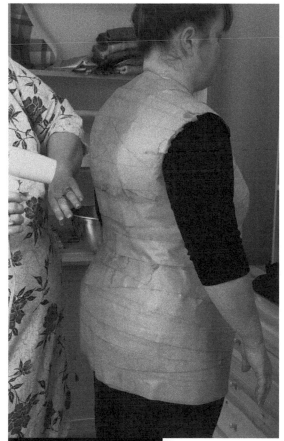

The outside layer of tape will lighten as it dries. Notice the darker areas on the back that are still quite wet.

You'll need strong hands and big scissors to liberate the wrapee when the tape is good and dry.

choosing fabric
for plus-sized designs

■ ■ 4 ■

When you walk into a fabric store, your senses of sight, touch, and even smell are immediately stimulated by the hundreds of colors, patterns, and textures that you see in the fabrics arrayed before you. Fabric is such a sensual pleasure! While the beauty of fabrics elicits a visceral and passionate response in most sewers, there is much more to fabric than meets the eye—or fingers and nose, for that matter. Plus-sized sewers must understand that the fiber content of the fabric that they choose affects the success or failure of each garment that they sew. Fabric choices affect a garment's design, durability, comfort, and care requirements.

■ FIBERS

Fibers are the smallest units from which fabrics are made. They are twisted together to form threads that are woven or knitted into fabrics. Every fiber has a characteristic set of performance properties, which affect your garment's success no matter what style of fabric those fibers are woven into. That's why the name of the fiber or fibers that make up a fabric is the most important piece of information that you need to consider before you purchase it.

Some of these performance characteristics have to do with aesthetics, the way a fabric made from a particular fiber looks. For example, the fabric's *hand* describes all its tactile qualities, that is, everything you can feel with your hand. Some qualities of hand are how smooth or textured the fabric is; its drape, or how softly or stiffly the fabric hangs when gathered; its luster, or how dull or shiny it is; and its wrinkle resistance.

Another performance characteristic that affects design is the fiber's durability. For exam-ple, some fibers are more resistant to abrasion than others, and some are stronger than others.

Comfort factors are also very important when selecting fibers for plus-sized designs. Some fibers are naturally absorbent and others are moisture repellent. A ripstop nylon that works well for a lightweight raincoat would not be comfortable for a warm weather night-gown. Some fibers breathe, that is, allow air and moisture to pass from the body to the outside air, or they may be occlusive, that is, hold in body heat and moisture.

Because each fiber differs in how it performs in terms of its aesthetics, durability, and comfort, you must determine the fiber content of every fabric you buy. This information should be written on the bolt end or on a tag attached to the roll of fabric.

Natural fibers

Generally, natural fibers are the best investment for plus-sized apparel. They are easier to sew because they press well, and they look and feel best on our plus-sized bodies.

There's more to fabrics than meets the eye. From the sheerest sheer to thick and textured, from restrained pin-stripes to hot pink, the options are almost limitless.

BURN TESTING

Federal laws require that all textiles be labeled with the generic or trade name of the fabric, the fiber content by percentages, and the country of origin. It's common practice, however, for stores to sell "mystery" fabrics with no labels or sometimes with labels that are incomplete or incorrect.

In better sewing stores, you can ask a clerk to burn-test a mystery fabric by snipping off a tiny swatch, holding it with tweezers over a metal pan or ashtray, and setting it on fire. Very generally speaking, protein fibers, such as silk and wool, smell like burned hair and leave a crushable black bead. Vegetable fibers, such as cotton, linen, or ramie, and cellulosic fibers, such as rayon or acetate, leave a fluffier ash and smell like burning paper. Most noncellulosic synthetics, on the other hand, usually leave a hard, plastic bead, which tells you what they're really made of.

If you find a fabric that is not labeled and the store will not burn test it, do not buy it! You won't know what you're paying for, and you won't know how the fabric will perform for your design.

WOOLENS AND WORSTEDS Woolens and worsteds are usually knitted or woven from the hairs of sheep. They usually require dry cleaning, but many knits, wovens that have been treated with special resins, and tightly woven twills like gabardine can be preshrunk, then hand-laundered in cold water, and hung or laid flat to dry.

Woolens are made from the shorter hairs of a fleece. They are warm, absorbent, bulky, and fuzzy. For these softer fabrics, pilling, abrasion, and felting from perspiration, body warmth, and pressure can be a problem, for example, on plus-sized pants at the upper, inner thigh. Luxury woolens are made from the hairs of other animals, including cashmere from a particular breed of goat, alpaca, camel hair, and angora from rabbit's fur.

Worsteds are woven from the longer fleece hairs from a higher twist yarn, which makes for

Natural fibers are the real thing. These are all wool, but they range from sturdy and tweedy to delicate and drapey.

a relatively finer, firmer thread. They are generally lighter in weight and thinner than woolens, are wiry, smooth, and slightly lustrous, and have a hard surface that wears very well. Worsteds make excellent jackets, skirts, and pants for plus sizes. They look classy, skim the body, resist wrinkling, breathe well even in tropical climates, and wear like iron.

SILK Silk is a protein fiber that is naturally spun by silkworms, just as a spider spins its web. Silk is luxurious and comfortable to wear, especially in hot and humid climates. Brightly colored silks or those used for heavily constructed garments like tailored jackets should be dry-cleaned. Silks in light colors or those used for simple garments can be hand-washed in cool

water and hung to dry, as has been done for the last 3,000 years of silk production.

Filament silk is made from very long, smooth silk fibers, so it's slippery and lustrous. Raw or noil silk is made from shorter pieces of silk

> tip *Some silks for closely fitted garments need to be underlined to avoid seam slippage. Seam slippage is that crosswise shredding that can occur at stressed vertical seams. To test for seam slippage, use your fingernail to scratch the fabric gently crosswise. If the threads shift easily from side to side, slippage is likely to occur.*

Filament silks are as vibrant as stained glass. Raw silks are as comfy as a cocoon.

fiber. It's much less expensive than filament silk and feels similar to cotton. Raw silk may abrade and pill because of the shorter fiber length, but it drapes, sews, and presses easily and makes beautiful, comfortable, and luxurious sportswear. For the last few years, all kinds of silk have been at their lowest prices in three decades, to the point that Chinese farmers are cutting down their mulberry trees (silkworms eat the leaves) to make way for more profitable crops. Take advantage of this market low, and choose silk over synthetics, which may cost no less than silk.

COTTON Cotton is comfortable and absorbent, drapes well, and varies widely in quality. Generally, look for a close weave and a long fiber length. Pull a thread from the cut end of

the cotton, untwist it, and look for fibers over 1 in. long.

Some cottons are heavily sized, or starched, to make them seem crisper, heavier, and more expensive, but of course the sizing will wash out when the fabric is laundered or dry-cleaned. Oftentimes you can hold a cotton up to the light and actually see particles of starch clinging between the warp and the weft. Most cottons launder well, but bright colors may fade, and many cottons may require ironing. Dry-clean cottons only if the construction is complicated, such as for a tailored jacket, or if the colors are bright, such as for a cerise pique evening dress. Dry-cleaning fluids are harsh on natural fibers and can leave residues (which are actually other people's dirt) that cause yellowing on whites and light colors. Cottons are an excellent choice for all kinds of plus-sized apparel.

LINEN Linen fibers come from the flax plant and have been around even longer than silk. Ancient Egyptian mummies were wound in strips of linen, some of which are still intact today. Linen is one of my favorite fibers for plus-sized designs. It is beautifully breathable and strong and wears very well. It's crisp, slightly lustrous, and luxurious. Linen fabrics vary in weight from transparent handkerchief linen to heavy upholstery fabrics. Look for a tight weave and avoid linens with heavy sizing.

Most linens for simpler garments and lighter colors can be hand-washed in cool water and hung to dry, while bright colors and complicated garments are best dry-cleaned. Linen softens with each washing and eventually develops an almost velvety patina. Yes, linen does wrinkle, which you can test by crushing the fabric in your hand. Often the wrinkles on heavier linen quickly fall out, and some linens have been treated with resins to resist creasing. To me, the "used handkerchief look" shouts luxury, so learn to love the wrinkles!

From gauze to suitings, crisp and cool linen is a prudent luxury.

> **tip** *Note that some fabrics and much ready-to-wear may be labeled "linen" but contain no flax fiber at all. They are simply cheaper, crisp, woven substitutes made of cotton, rayon, or polyester, or they may be blends with a small percentage of flax.*

Other plant fibers such as hemp, ramie, and jute function similarly to linen, but their fibers may be relatively shorter than those of other vegetable fabrics, so they may not wear as well. You can pull a fiber from the cut end of the piece to test it as you can with cotton.

Synthetics

Man-made fibers are identified by their fiber name, trade name, or the manufacturing process used to turn the basic fiber into a fabric. Most synthetics were developed to replace more costly or less available natural fibers.

RAYON One of the oldest synthetic fibers is rayon, which was first made from the cellulose in wood pulp in 1889 as a substitute for silk, linen, wool, and cotton. It was widely used during and after both WWI and WWII when sources for natural fibers were disrupted. Rayon fabrics are strong when dry but weak when wet. They are breathable, resist abrasion, and drape attractively. They also shrink when laundered, and most wrinkle very badly.

Viscose rayon tends to wrinkle the most of all the rayon manufacturing processes. Cuprammonium rayon uses copper compounds to dissolve the cellulose; it is a relatively finer fiber that is crisper and more drapable, launders more easily, and does not wrinkle as much as viscose rayon. Bemberg lining fabrics are an example of this type of rayon. Polynosic rayon is completely washable and has a hand similar to high quality cotton. Tencel is a trade name for a rayon similar to polynosic rayon, which is manufactured by a fairly new process in the United States.

> ## tip
> *Since many fabrics labeled "rayon" do not specify what type of rayon, it's sometimes hard to guess how they will perform. When in doubt, buy ¼ yard and preshrink the swatch before you buy more. A crisp, tweedy suiting may work fine if it is underlined and dry-cleaned, but it could change to a wrinkly, soft, gauzy mess after washing.*

ACETATE Acetate was also developed as a silk substitute; it is often used for bridal, evening, and lining fabrics. It is also a cellulosic fiber made by dissolving cellulose from wood pulp in acetone. That's why acetate will dissolve in acetone nail polish remover. Acetate is usually dry-cleaned and may water-spot from perspiration or during steam pressing from errant drips. However, it is lustrous and crisp, comfortable and breathable, so it is an excellent choice for plus-sized eveningwear and linings.

ACRYLIC Acrylic fiber was developed as a substitute for woolens, and it is often seen in the form of knits and fleece fabrics. Acrylics are warm, bulky, fuzzy, stretchy, and comfortable to wear and can be easily washed. Because this fiber is soft, it pills easily and also holds static.

NYLON Nylon, also a substitute for silk, is usually slippery and very strong and drapes well, but it is also occlusive and has a very low melt temperature, so it doesn't take a press very well. Nylons range in use from bulletproof ballistic cloth to Cordura luggage fabric to the sheerest of panty hose. Because most nylons do not breathe, you may wish to avoid them for most garments. Some of the newer types of nylon, such as Taslan or Supplex, are more comfortable and make excellent lightweight, windproof, and water-repellent outerwear for plus sizes.

SPANDEX Spandex, also tradenamed Lycra and Glospan, was developed as a substitute for rubber after WWII. Spandex is usually covered with other fibers such as cotton, nylon, silk, or wool to produce blends for knitted and woven fabrics. A little spandex in a fabric adds stretch for shapewear, increases movement for active sportswear, and adds comfort and body to all fabrics. Never use chlorine bleach on any fabric containing spandex—it will yellow and deteriorate the fiber.

POLYESTER Polyester, a.k.a. "The Famous Twin Sisters Polly and Esther," is really a form of plastic made from petroleum products. Polyesters are wrinkle resistant, durable, cheap, widely available, and attractive looking, but they do not breathe. They are extremely unabsorbent and uncomfortable to wear, especially for large, warm people. Wearing a polyester blouse or lining next to your skin, particularly in hot and humid climates, can make you feel as if you're wrapped in plastic wrap, which is indeed the case.

Although polyester can be washed and dried, it also attracts body and food oils like a magnet. They may not launder out, thus the dreaded "ring around the collar" that can develop on polyester or polyester-blend shirts. Because polyester doesn't press well, it is also more difficult to sew than a natural fiber. Please avoid polyester for your everyday garments. When you need to wear a garment for only a couple of hours at a time in a climate-controlled environment such as in the evening, polyesters are fine; otherwise, they will make you look and feel miserable.

Blends combine both the best and worst of their components' performance characteristics. A cotton/polyester blend, for example, may make you feel sticky and will hold oil stains, but it won't wrinkle as much as all cotton. Blends also pill more easily than single fiber fabrics because different fibers may not stay twisted together and may break loose to form pills.

■ MAKING YOUR FABRIC CHOICE

Once you have determined the fiber content of a fabric and have thought about that fiber's performance characteristics, consider how its drape, color, texture, and pattern will affect your garment's design. For example, will a knit be unattractively clingy, or will it skim the body? Will a sheer make you feel embarrassed and conspicuous or feminine and sexy?

What the pattern suggests

Check the back of the pattern for fabric suggestions, paying attention to the warnings about what kinds of fabrics are unsuitable. However, you can also have fun breaking the rules! When you use fabrics other than those recommended, what you change in terms of design are actually the surface characteristics. The results can be either disastrous or stunningly original. For example, I have a photo from a fashion magazine of an exquisitely pricey designer jacket made of saffron silk organza, with all the expensive hand-tailored, pad-stitched canvas and taping showing through the sheer fabric on the lapel, adding to the design. Likewise, a shirtwaist dress might look tailored and professional in a crisp, cotton shirting but could look sexy and swingy in a soft, fluid silk crepe de chine.

Durability and care

Durability and care requirements are also important factors for plus-sized designs. For pants, hard-surfaced fabrics such as worsteds, linens, closely woven cottons, and yes, polyesters, are better than fuzzy woolens, inexpensive rayons, or fluffy acrylics.

Remember that the time and money you invest in your wardrobe will be worthwhile if your garments wear well for many years. If you can't abide wrinkles and hate to iron, choose fibers or resin-treated fabrics with wrinkle resistance. I have made rayon outfits, for example, that look and feel fabulous and have precipitated many compliments, but I have to iron them after each wearing. I don't have the time, and I'm too cheap to have them dry-cleaned, so they hang in my closet. Also, if you sweat heavily, avoid filament silks and acetates, if they water-spot, as well as nonbreathable fibers, such as nylon and polyester.

■ UNDERLININGS, LININGS, AND INTERFACINGS FOR PLUS-SIZED DESIGNS

Once you have chosen the fashion fabric that shows on the outside of your garment, you need to select additional fabrics for the inside of your garment. Fabrics for underlinings and interfacings provide essential support to shape the fashion fabric into the design of the garment. Underlinings or linings finish the inside neatly and make a garment more comfortable to wear. I cover the application of underlinings on p. 107. While you're selecting fashion fabric, check the yardage requirements

Lining is as important as face fabric. Make your lining choice part of your garment plan, not an afterthought.

on the back of the pattern for the other fabrics that you might need.

Underlining

An underlining is simply an extra fabric layer that is cut and stitched as one with the face fabric. Underlining fabrics can include sheath lining, taffeta, China silk, organza, batiste, cotton flannel, tulle, crepe de chine, crinoline net, muslin, and many more, all from a variety of fibers and blends. Try different underlinings with your fabric to obtain the resulting hand that you desire. Match care requirements and performance qualities of your underlining to your face fabric.

Lining

Lining fabrics should be opaque, slightly crisp, slippery, and closely woven. Choose silk crepe de chine or charmeuse for luxury garments or acetate sheath linings, satin, or taffeta for moderate value garments. Bemberg

PRETREATING YOUR FABRIC

You must always preshrink all your fabrics, underlinings, linings, and trims before cutting and sewing. Do not skip this step, or you will regret it later. When you launder or steam-press dry-clean-only garments, all the components of the garment will shrink at different rates if they have not been preshrunk. That's why garments sometimes wrinkle and pucker after laundering around zippers, trim, and interfaced areas.

Preshrinking also removes sizing so you will know what the fabric will feel and look like after laundering.

If washable, pink or serge the cut ends of the fabric to prevent raveling, and then wash and dry it the same way you will launder the completed garment. Dry-clean-only fabrics need to be steam-pressed to preshrink them.

is a high-quality rayon that comes in two weights and is excellent. Please do not use cheap polyester and nylon linings, particularly for natural fiber garments. They do not press well and will make you look and feel hot and uncomfortable.

Interfacing

Interfacings are also crucial to your garment's success. Always test them: Layer a scrap of your face fabric with a swatch of interfacing, fuse it carefully according to the manufacturer's instructions if it is fusible, and judge the resulting hand. When possible, match the performance properties of an interfacing's fiber with that of the face fabric; it doesn't make much sense to fuse an underlining of nylon tricot to a wool crepe jacket, for example, because the nylon will make the jacket less breathable. Always buy the best quality interfacing you can afford, and avoid the cheap, crafty kind that comes precut in plastic bags.

■ THE QUEST FOR QUALITY

Always buy the best quality materials you can afford. Remember, a fine fabric and simple design look better than a cheap fabric and an elaborate design. Also, it makes no sense to invest your valuable time and labor in cheap fabrics that may not perform the way you need them to or remain wearable for very long.

If you have a hard time judging fabric quality, do some free snooping in an expensive boutique or department store. Be sure to dress well! Check out the fiber content labels for face and lining fabrics, and flip garments inside out to examine construction techniques. How do these vary from budget apparel?

Often, the mill name printed on the selvage is a sign of quality. If the name of the manufacturer is woven into the selvage or if decorative contrast threads are woven into the selvage, the fabric is nearly always of good quality. Price is often, but not always, an indication of quality. Usually, moderately priced fabrics are perfectly fine, but the cheapest may be no bargain because of low quality.

In addition to local sewing stores, you can subscribe to swatching services. For a small fee, you get a number of mailings a year with swatches to examine. You can even test these swatches for slippage and launder them to test for wrinkling and shrinking. I find swatching services a tremendous time-saver; I'd rather spend my time sewing than shopping! Also, these services frequently offer coordinates, so you can buy coordinated fabric for a season's wardrobe with only one phone call and a credit card.

Many cities and towns have garment or textile factories that may sell leftover fabrics or mill ends. Some of these factories are squirreled away, even in the hinterlands, not just in big cities. You can find out about these from word of mouth, or you can check a Business to Business Yellow Pages at your library.

You can also buy fabric when you travel. Then you will get to wear your souvenirs!

adjusting the pattern to fit your body size

▪ ▪ 5 ▪

If you're a plus-sized sewer with a sense of style, you've probably lusted after many of the licensed designer patterns available from the major pattern companies, or you may have hankered after a historical or ethnic design from a small pattern company. Unfortunately, many of these patterns run only to a size 16 or 18. Copying these designs with flat pattern drafting works fine in plus sizes if you have plenty of time and pattern drafting skills.

A commercial pattern, on the other hand, is a tremendous time-saver. Even though you need to adjust the pattern to fit your body, all the rest of the drafting work is already done for you. To me, it makes much more sense to pay $10 to $20 for a designer pattern, which is an exact copy of the toile (muslin test garment) used to manufacture clothing that may cost thousands, than it is to spend many hours custom drafting either by hand or computer, cutting a muslin, and fitting that muslin before even starting on the actual garment. So when your big and beautiful size 24 daughter wants an Alicyn wedding dress that only goes to an 18, or you can't live without the Lagerfeld suit with its wonderfully tricky seaming that is only available two sizes too small, or the Tamotsu career wardrobe that would be perfect for the office goes up to a 24 but you're a 32, what's a plus-sized sewer to do?

Over the years, for myself and particularly for my custom clothing customers, I have developed a simple technique for enlarging patterns that I call "sizing up." This method is fast and easy, and it maintains original design lines. To understand how and why it works, it helps to know how both the ready-to-wear industry and the pattern companies size their patterns.

■ STANDARDIZED SIZING IS A MISNOMER

Manufacturers of plus-sized apparel assume that a particular set of measurements corresponds with their intended customer's body shape, and this is usually an apple-shaped figure. That's why ready-to-wear in plus sizes is often huge across the shoulders and bust and too small across the hips, particularly for pear-shaped, plus-sized women; we come in a variety of basic body shapes, not just one.

To make larger-sized garments, the factory patternmaker uses a standardized chart to slash each pattern piece in several places, both horizontally and vertically, and then spreads them by prescribed increments. This process is called pattern grading (see the drawing below). Grading patterns increases the overall dimensions of a pattern piece without distorting the overall shape of that piece or the design of the garment. Grading can be done manually or by computer.

Pattern companies enlarge patterns in the same manner, but they use a set of measurements based on 30-year-old data, which in turn is based on 50-year-old data. Yet with subsequent generations, women in general have grown taller and bigger, which is why so few daughters can fit into their mothers' wedding gowns!

So the standardized measurement numbers used by clothing manufacturers and pattern companies to grade up to plus sizes help to market clothes and patterns, and they help us figure out what size to start with. However, these numbers are often merely arithmetical extrapolations from one small size, and they may have little to do with the measurements of real people. It's very rare for an individual's actual body measurements to conform both vertically and horizontally to those of a standardized size. Furthermore, almost no one has an idealized body shaped like a dress form without any figure variations. That's why nearly no one can pull a pattern out of the envelope, cut and sew the garment, and expect it to fit well.

This is especially true for large women. The grading process assumes that bodies and their skeletal frames increase proportionally and regularly from size to size. In fact, real large women are usually relatively larger in the neck, upper arms, midriff, bust, and hip but may not be proportionally larger in shoulder length, lower arms, legs, and so on. Every body is unique, and we come in pear, potato, and Madam Peanut shapes as well as in apple shapes. We don't all get taller as we get bigger, either! This is why both ready-to-wear and patterns for plus sizes tend to be too long in

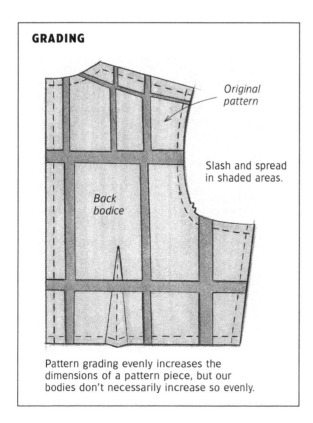

GRADING

Original pattern

Slash and spread in shaded areas.

Back bodice

Pattern grading evenly increases the dimensions of a pattern piece, but our bodies don't necessarily increase so evenly.

the shoulder length, sleeve length, and other lengths as well. Sizing may be standard, but people are not.

Unlike pattern grading, which enlarges uniformly from one standardized size to the next, my technique of sizing up only enlarges the pattern exactly where the wearer needs it. This method takes you from a standardized size to your unique body size.

■ YOUR BODY ISN'T IDEAL, IT'S REAL: SIZING UP

Because your figure is not the same as an idealized figure, you absolutely must take the time to calculate how much the measurements for a standardized pattern vary from your actual body measurements in both length and width (see "How to Take Your Measurements" on pp. 58-59). You also must determine where these variations occur on your body and make the corresponding adjustments on your pattern

tip   *I talked to a plastic surgeon once who confided that the most common reason her patients cited for seeking cosmetic surgery was so their clothes would fit better. Too bad these women don't sew or use dressmakers! Good sewing isn't easy, but it's certainly easier than pain, scars, and doctors' bills!*

before you cut out the garment. Once you've made these simple calculations, you will be able to adjust a pattern easily and accurately.

Basic width adjustments

Start by comparing your body measurements with those on the back of the pattern, on the envelope flap, or printed with the instructions. Note the differences—plus or minus—at the

SELECTING YOUR BEST PATTERN SIZE

Since the bust area is usually more complicated to adjust than other body areas, use your bust measurement for blouses, dresses, and ensembles if you are an A to B cup size. If you are a C cup or larger or if you have a small skeletal frame, use your chest measurement as if it were your bust measurement. This will allow a better fit through the shoulders and upper chest after you make the adjustments described in this chapter.

For skirts and pants, use your full hip measurement. If you are in between sizes, which is very common, pick the larger size. It's easier to take in a garment during fitting than to let it out, so always err on the side of largeness. If there is complicated construction detail in a particular area of the garment, use the closest measurement for that area. For example, for a dress with diagonal color blocking over the chest and your measurements are 46-44-50, use the bust measure-

ment to select a size 24 with measurements of 46−39−48 to reduce the need for pattern adjustments in a complicated area of the design.

If you are larger than the pattern's size range, just buy the largest size. As you'll learn, it's easy to adjust a pattern to fit your unique size and to size up to larger sizes that will fit you.

WIDTH ADJUSTMENTS EXAMPLE
(in inches)

	STANDARDIZED SIZE 24 MEASUREMENTS	ACTUAL BODY MEASUREMENTS	TOTAL CHANGE
Bust	46	52	+ 6
Waist	39	47	+ 8
Hip	48	55	+ 7

bust, waist, and full hip. It's very common for women to be larger than average at one point on their bodies and smaller than average at others, so don't be concerned if you have both pluses and minuses.

Next, count the number of vertical seam edges, excluding the center front and center back. For example, a dart-fitted bodice would have two side seams with 2 edges each, or a total of 4 edges. A princess-lined bodice would have two side seams and four princess seams, or 12 edges. Pants typically have two side seams, or 4 edges. A six-gore skirt would have two side seams plus four princess seams, or 12 edges.

Then divide the total width to be added or subtracted by the number of edges. Note that the total width to be added or subtracted may vary from bust to waist to hips. For an example, see the chart "Width Adjustments Example" above.

In this example, for a dart-fitted bodice with 4 edges on two side seams, you would need to add 1½ in. at the bust, 2 in. at the waist, and 1¾ in. at the hip. Likewise, for a princess-

seamed bodice with 12 edges, you would need to add ½ in. at the bust, ⅔ in. at the waist, and about ⅝ in. at the hips. If you come up with an odd fraction like ⁷⁄₁₂, just round up to a larger fraction that's easier to measure.

You can use the chart "Basic Size Adjustments in Width" on p. 60 to help calculate the increases or decreases you may need in width.

Once you've calculated the necessary increases, use a ruler to mark points every 1 in. to 2 in. parallel to the old cutting lines, blending between body areas as increases or decreases vary.

Many skilled sewers, patternmakers, and educators have developed a variety of measuring techniques. They may measure different parts of the body in different ways. While all of these systems are useful and valid if used consistently, my method uses easy-to-locate anatomical points without marking the body or locating imaginary lines. Note that these measurements are useful for adjusting commercial patterns, not necessarily for drafting patterns.

Preparation

While it's most accurate to have a friend measure you, you can do it yourself if your arms are flexible enough. Start by wearing the undergarments and heel height you'll wear with the garment you plan to sew; heel height affects posture, which affects fit. Stand and breathe normally; do not lock your knees or suck in your gut! Tie a string or narrow ribbon around your waist (yes, you do have one—it's in there somewhere), and check in a mirror that the string is parallel to the floor. If you are large-busted, stick a piece of tape from apex to apex to form a bridge across the breasts, since most bodices drape over the bust apexes, not between the breasts.

For horizontal measurements, hold the tape parallel to the floor; for vertical ones, hold it perpendicular. Since the softer areas of your body are compressible, try to exert a consistent degree of pressure on the tape as you hold it around the body; the tape measure should be comfortably snug and not so loose that it droops unevenly. Remember to keep your fingers outside of the tape: Do not measure your fingers! Take and record your measurements as listed in "Personal Body Measurement Chart" on the facing page and as shown in the drawing below.

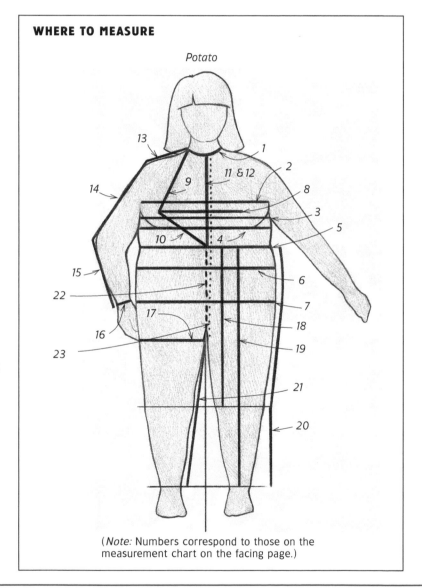

WHERE TO MEASURE

Potato

(*Note:* Numbers correspond to those on the measurement chart on the facing page.)

PERSONAL BODY MEASUREMENT CHART

Note: Numbers correspond with the drawing on the facing page.

* measurement not shown on drawing

1. **Neck:** at the base, where a jewel neckline would fall _____

2. **Chest:** under the arms and above the bust _____

3. **Bust:** across the fullest part and across the bridge _____

4. **Midriff:** just below the bust _____

5. **Waist:** where the string is _____

6. **High hip:** about 3 in. below your waistline _____

7. **Full hip:** wherever you are widest, which may be across your thighs _____

8. **Bust apex to apex:** straight across the bridge _____

9. **Side neck to bust apex:** from the base of the neck at the shoulder seam to the apex on the same side

of the body _____

10. **Bust apex to CF waist:** measure diagonally to the string at CF _____

11. **Front waist length:** from the base of the neck at CF, over the bridge, to the string _____

12. **Back waist length*:** from the prominent bone at the base of the neck at CB to the string _____

13. **Shoulder length:** from the base of the neck at the shoulder seam position to the prominent bone at the

shoulder, where a natural shoulder line would fall _____

14. **Shoulder to elbow:** from the prominent bone at the natural shoulder line to the bony tip of the

elbow _____

15. **Elbow to wrist:** from the point of the elbow to just below the wrist bone _____

16. **Wrist:** _____

17. **Thigh:** wherever it is widest _____

18. **Waist front to below knee:** from the string to the bottom of the kneecap _____

19. **Waist front to floor:** _____

20. **Outseam:** from the string at the side seam to your desired pants length _____

21. **Inseam:** from the top of your inner thigh to your desired pants length _____

22. **Crotch length*:** from the string at center back, through the legs, and up to

the string at CF _____

23. **Body length*:** from the base of the neck at CB through the legs and up to the base of the neck

at CF _____

BASIC SIZE ADJUSTMENTS IN WIDTH				
(in inches)				
	STANDARDIZED MEASUREMENT FOR SIZE	ACTUAL BODY MEASUREMENT	DIFFERENCE + OR −	NO. OF VERTICAL EDGES (WITH/ WITHOUT CF & CB)	AMOUNT ADJUSTMENT PER EDGE
Bust					
Waist					
Hip					
You must also add wearing and designer ease, as described on p. 72.					

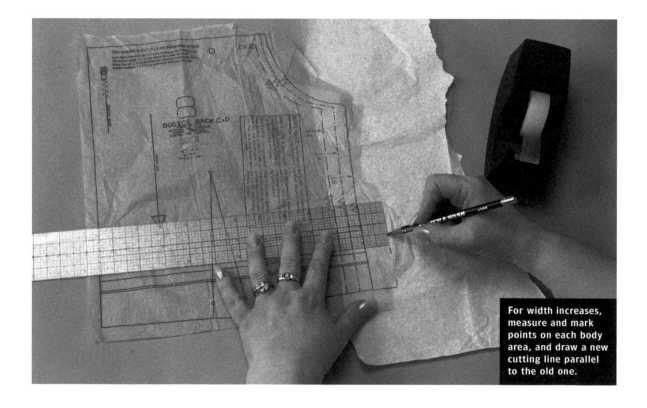

For width increases, measure and mark points on each body area, and draw a new cutting line parallel to the old one.

Connect the dots to form the new cutting lines (see the photo above). Or use a transparent, gridded ruler to line up the old cutting line with the grid or slot on the ruler that corresponds to the desired increase, and draw the new line, pivoting the ruler as you draw to follow curves.

Tape tissue, strips of drafting paper, or pieces of adding machine tape (which is maddeningly curly but a convenient width) to the seamlines as needed. Because these paper extensions may dull your sewing shears, trim around the cutting lines of each piece with paper scissors before you cut your fabric.

If you need to increase any torso widths more than about 10 in., then include the center front and center back lines as 4 more edges, and adjust them, too. This helps maintain design proportions. For example, to add 10 in. to a princess-lined bodice, count center front and center back as 4 edges, two side seams as 4 edges, and four princess seams as 8 edges, which is 16 edges total, or about ⅝ in. per edge. Maintain the center front and center back as foldlines or cutting lines.

Plus-sized women are generally less proportionally large across their chests than across their lower torsos. So, if you have increased the bust area, add width to the front and back pat-

> **tip**   *For a garment with a wide neckline, you may need to prevent the neck opening from becoming too large. If you need to add more than 10 in. in width to a garment with two side seams and four edges, you may wish to add less of the total width increase at the center front and center back than at the side seam edges. For example, to add 10 in. of width, you could add ½ in. to the four edges at center front and center back and then add 2 in. at each side seam edge to avoid distortion of the neckline.*

INCREASING BODICE WIDTH

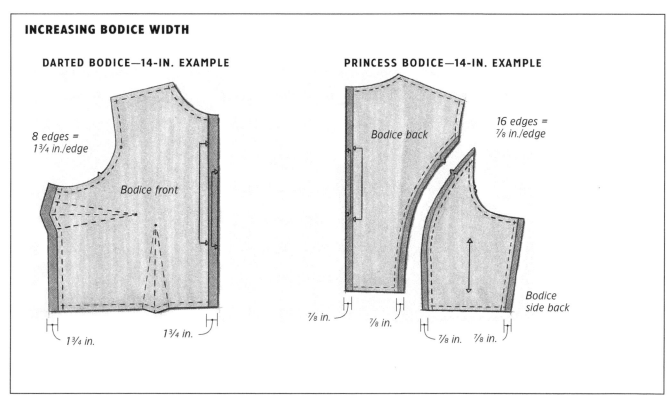

DARTED BODICE—14-IN. EXAMPLE

8 edges = 1¾ in./edge

Bodice front

1¾ in.   1¾ in.

PRINCESS BODICE—14-IN. EXAMPLE

Bodice back

16 edges = ⅞ in./edge

Bodice side back

⅞ in.   ⅞ in.   ⅞ in.   ⅞ in.

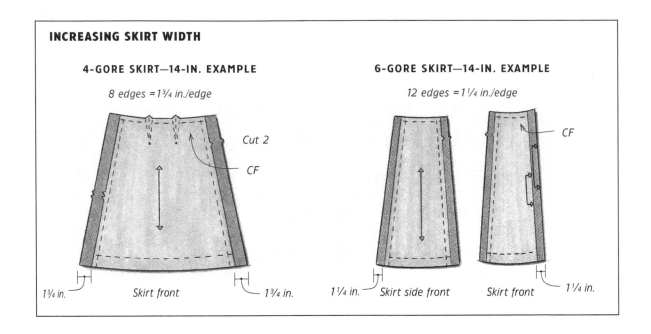

INCREASING SKIRT WIDTH

4-GORE SKIRT—14-IN. EXAMPLE

8 edges = 1¾ in./edge

Cut 2

CF

1¾ in.   Skirt front   1¾ in.

6-GORE SKIRT—14-IN. EXAMPLE

12 edges = 1¼ in./edge

CF

1¼ in.   Skirt side front   Skirt front   1¼ in.

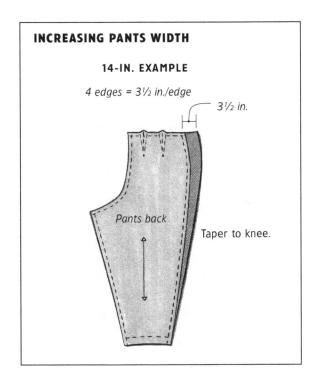

INCREASING PANTS WIDTH

14-IN. EXAMPLE

4 edges = 3½ in./edge

3½ in.

Pants back

Taper to knee.

cumference by 4 in., then add one-quarter the amount of *one* of those increases, or ¼ in., to the width across the chest and back at each armscye. Connect the new side seam cutting line to the new armscye cutting line, and then add the increase, starting just below the notch and tapering to nothing at the shoulder seam.

This works with princess seams as well. When you increase width at princess seams, you also widen across the upper torso, so one-quarter of the relatively smaller increase in width that you added at *one* side seam is adequate to widen the garment across the front and back at the armscye. If you don't make this adjustment, the sleeve cap will form a horizontal stress line from notch to notch, and arm movement would be restricted. If the chest area ends up too wide at the armscye, it will be easy to pin out during a first fitting (see Chapter 8 beginning on p. 122).

tern pieces at the armscye area by about one-quarter of the increase at *one* side seam. For example, if you added 1 in. to each of the side seams at the bust to increase the total bust cir-

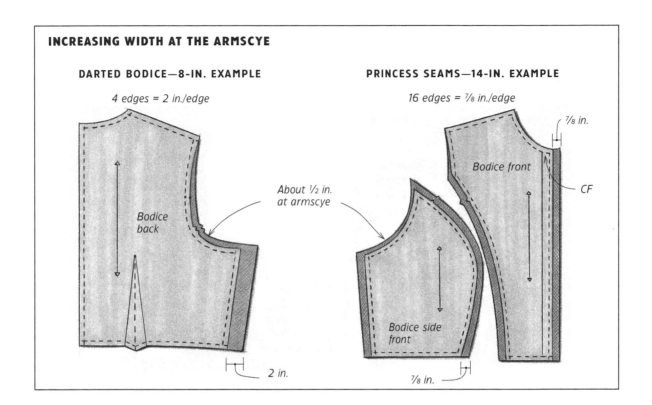

INCREASING WIDTH AT THE ARMSCYE

DARTED BODICE—8-IN. EXAMPLE

4 edges = 2 in./edge

Bodice back

About ½ in. at armscye

2 in.

PRINCESS SEAMS—14-IN. EXAMPLE

16 edges = ⅞ in./edge

⅞ in.

Bodice front

CF

Bodice side front

⅞ in.

Complex width adjustments

Sizing up some types of garments requires a bit more endeavor and creativity. Because these wild and wonderful designs are exciting to sew and aesthetically satisfying to wear, they are often worth the slightly extra effort.

GEOMETRIC OR ASYMMETRICAL SEAMING Garments with geometric or asymmetrical seaming should be adjusted so as not to distract from the design (see the top drawings on p. 64); how you do this will vary with each garment. For example, for a chemise with diagonal color blocking, you can adjust at the side seams only. If you need to add more than 10 in. and the diagonal lines meet at center front, you can slash and spread the center front and center back and extend the diagonal lines to fit the pieces of the color blocking together. If you must disturb geometrically intersecting seamlines, it is best to test your adjustments in muslin first.

GARMENTS WITHOUT SIDE SEAMS Some garments do not have side seams, including many geometrically or asymmetrically seamed designs. For these, you need to slash and spread all the corresponding pieces wherever an adjustment will least disturb the design (see the bottom drawing on p. 64 and the top drawing on p. 65); that place will likely change with each individual garment. You can adjust some garments, such as sweatpants or palazzo pants without side seams, where the side seam would ordinarily be by slashing and spreading one-half the total circumference increase at each side seam area.

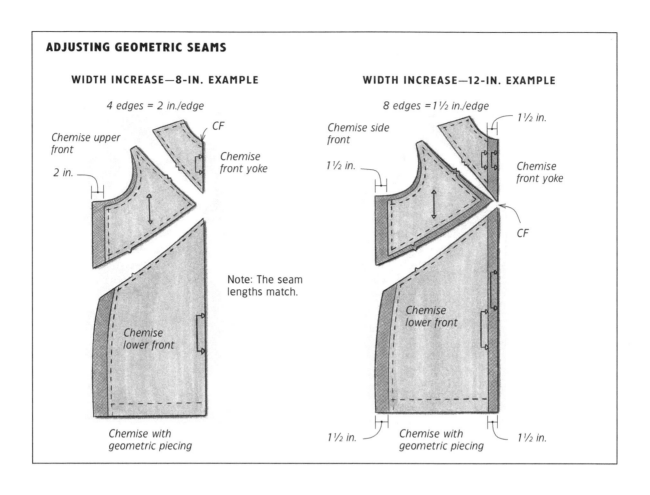

ADJUSTING GEOMETRIC SEAMS

WIDTH INCREASE—8-IN. EXAMPLE

4 edges = 2 in./edge

Chemise upper front

2 in.

CF

Chemise front yoke

Note: The seam lengths match.

Chemise lower front

Chemise with geometric piecing

WIDTH INCREASE—12-IN. EXAMPLE

8 edges = 1½ in./edge

1½ in.

Chemise side front

1½ in.

Chemise front yoke

CF

Chemise lower front

1½ in.   Chemise with   1½ in.
                geometric piecing

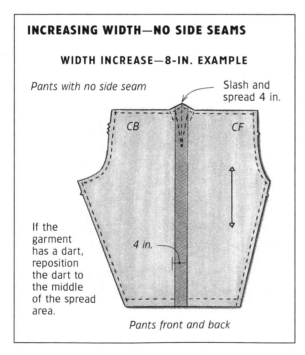

INCREASING WIDTH—NO SIDE SEAMS

WIDTH INCREASE—8-IN. EXAMPLE

Pants with no side seam

Slash and spread 4 in.

CB   CF

If the garment has a dart, reposition the dart to the middle of the spread area.

4 in.

Pants front and back

CIRCULAR GARMENTS Circular garments, such as full-, half-, or gored circle skirts, circular capes, and some circular cocoon wraps need to be increased in width by lowering the waist or neck cutting line (see the bottom drawings on the facing page). The pieces of a circular garment are sectors of a circle, and the waistline or neckline and hemline are arcs of that circle. So if you lower the waist arc, you increase its length. Use your tape measure on its side to find the right arc position for your waist measurement; then carefully draw the new arc parallel to the old one. If needed to maintain garment length, lower the hemline arc by the same amount.

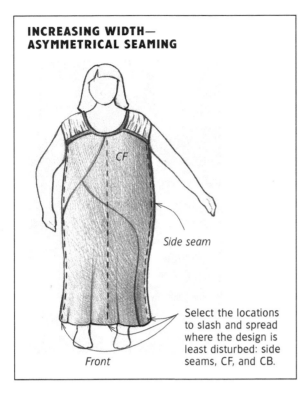
Circle skirts that are gathered at the waist or gathered or pleated onto a hip yoke may be alternatively adjusted for width along the entire length of the seams.

> **tip** *Circle skirts often use big pieces of fabric. Depending on the design and your size, you may need to piece your fabric or create more seams. For example, a full-circle skirt designed with two side seams could be sewn as a full-circle, four-gore skirt by changing the foldline to a cutting line and adding a seam allowance (see the center drawing below).*

ADJUSTING CIRCLE SKIRTS

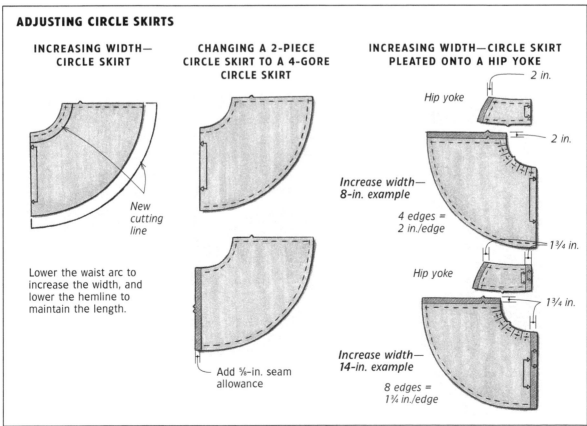

**INCREASING WIDTH—
CIRCLE SKIRT**

New
cutting
line

Lower the waist arc to
increase the width, and
lower the hemline to
maintain the length.

**CHANGING A 2-PIECE
CIRCLE SKIRT TO A 4-GORE
CIRCLE SKIRT**

Add ⅝-in. seam
allowance

**INCREASING WIDTH—CIRCLE SKIRT
PLEATED ONTO A HIP YOKE**

Hip yoke

2 in.

2 in.

*Increase width—
8-in. example*

4 edges =
2 in./edge

1¾ in.

Hip yoke

1¾ in.

*Increase width—
14-in. example*

8 edges =
1¾ in./edge

Adjust all the corresponding pieces

Once you have the overall widths of the main pattern pieces adjusted, you need to evaluate all the other pieces so they fit with the main pattern pieces to fit your body.

JEWEL NECKLINES Hold a tape measure on its side to measure the length of the front and back neck stitching lines; compare this measurement to your neck measurement. A jewel neckline needs about 1 in. of ease. You can either scoop the neckline lower and wider for comfort or add length at the shoulder seams (see the drawings below). For example, two shoulder seams make four edges, so for a 2-in. increase, you add ½ in. to each seam edge. If you have already adjusted the center front and center back lines, be sure to include their width when measuring. Any excess in the shoulder or vari-

ations in shoulder slope can be pinned out later during a fitting.

ONE-PIECE SLEEVES If you increased the bustline width at the side seams, you must add the same amount to the upper sleeve seam so the pieces will fit together (see the top drawing on the facing page). Add the same width increase to each side of the sleeve seam that you added to the front and back side seams of the bodice, using a ruler to taper to nothing at the elbow, since plus-sized arms are usually wider in the upper arm area only. Measure the new width of the upper sleeve and compare to your upper arm measurement, allowing at least 2 in. for wearing ease.

TWO-PIECE SLEEVES Slash and spread the under-sleeve vertically at the underarm mark, spread at the armscye seam the total amount of the

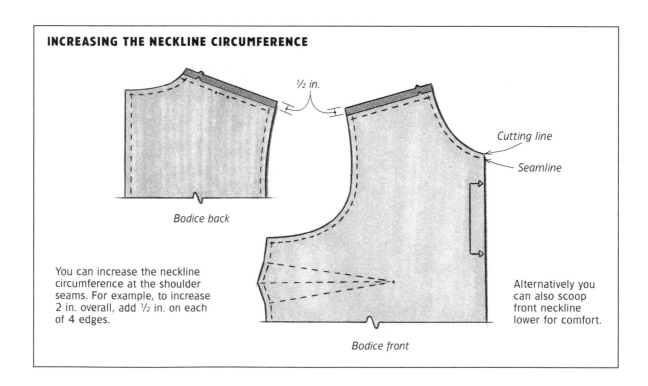

INCREASING THE NECKLINE CIRCUMFERENCE

½ in.

Bodice back

You can increase the neckline circumference at the shoulder seams. For example, to increase 2 in. overall, add ½ in. on each of 4 edges.

Cutting line

Seamline

Alternatively you can also scoop front neckline lower for comfort.

Bodice front

ADJUSTING SLEEVES

INCREASING WIDTH—1-PIECE SLEEVE

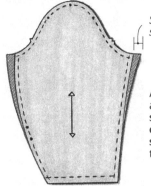

Same as one side seam increase

Add the same amount as the side seam increase to each edge of the sleeve seam; taper to elbow.

INCREASING WIDTH—2-PIECE SLEEVE

Increase width of a 2-piece sleeve at the side seam (underarm).

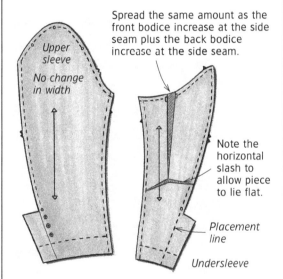

Upper sleeve

No change in width

Spread the same amount as the front bodice increase at the side seam plus the back bodice increase at the side seam.

Note the horizontal slash to allow piece to lie flat.

Placement line

Undersleeve

ADJUSTING THE SLEEVE CAP

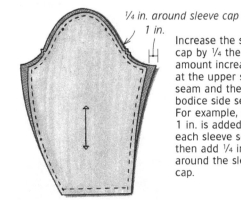

¼ in. around sleeve cap

1 in.

Increase the sleeve cap by ¼ the amount increased at the upper sleeve seam and the bodice side seams. For example, if 1 in. is added at each sleeve seam, then add ¼ in. around the sleeve cap.

increases at the front and back bodice side seams, and tape to a tissue underlay (see the center drawing at left).

SLEEVE CAPS Large arms are rounder and therefore longer and wider across the sleeve cap than average-sized arms. For both one-piece and two-piece sleeves, you must also increase both the width and the length of the sleeve cap by the same amount you added to the armscye at the shoulder seam, front and back at the chest, and the underarm (see the bottom drawing at left). If you do not, the sleeve cap will be too narrow and short and will form unattractive and uncomfortable horizontal stress lines from notch to notch.

Draw a new cutting line from just below the notch, parallel to the old cutting line, and about one-quarter the increase at *one* side seam. If you want to measure, you should generally have about 2 in. of ease between the length of the armscye seamline on the bodice and on the sleeve. If the sleeve cap is too big, it's easy to pin out the excess later.

COLLARS, NECK FACINGS, AND OTHER CONNECTING PIECES If you have adjusted the pattern at the shoulder seams, center front, or center back, you must also slash and spread the same amount at the same locations as you did when you adjusted the neck seamline. All other connecting pieces of the pattern need corresponding horizontal increases in the same manner. For example, for a chemise with a front diagonal drape, remember to increase the width of the drape in the same manner as you did the dress front. Double-check that you have

ADJUSTING THE COLLAR AND NECK FACINGS

Adjust the collar, facings, and other corresponding pieces.

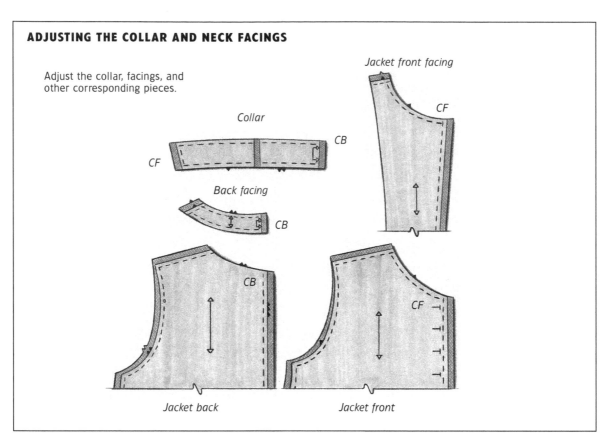

Jacket front facing

Collar

CF

CB

CF

Back facing

CB

CB

CF

Jacket back

Jacket front

ADJUSTING A FRONT DRAPE

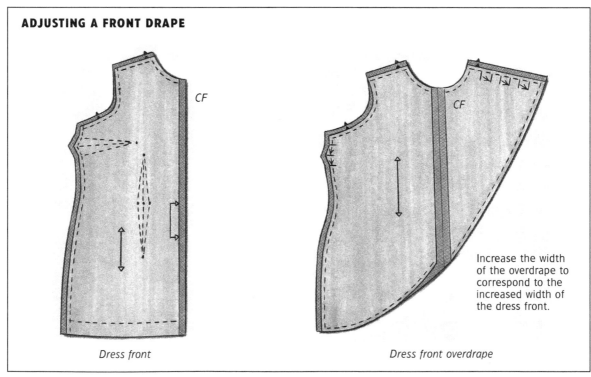

CF

CF

Increase the width of the overdrape to correspond to the increased width of the dress front.

Dress front

Dress front overdrape

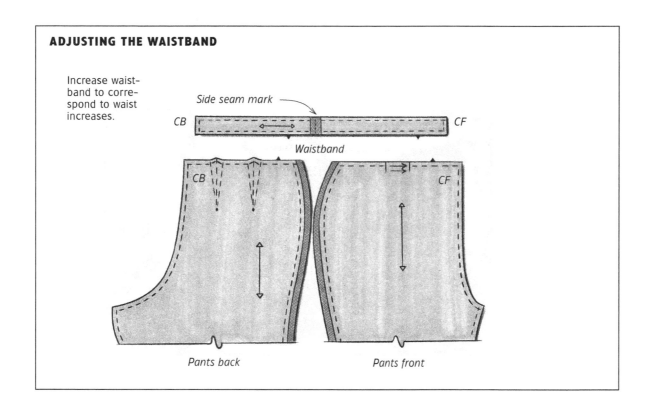

ADJUSTING THE WAISTBAND

Increase waistband to correspond to waist increases.

Side seam mark

CB   CF

Waistband

CB   CF

Pants back   *Pants front*

adjusted all yokes, facings, collars, waistband, contrast bands, and so on in the same places and by the same amount so that all the pattern pieces fit together during construction.

Length adjustments

Compare vertical measurements on the pattern piece to your own for the back and front waist length, sleeve length, skirt or pant length, and so on. Use the waistline mark on the pattern piece as a reference. Large women are round rather than angular, therefore they are proportionally longer as well as wider than average. On the other hand, standardized sizing assumes we're all 6 ft. tall, so don't be surprised if you shorten below the waist and lengthen above, or vice versa. Use the chart "Basic Size

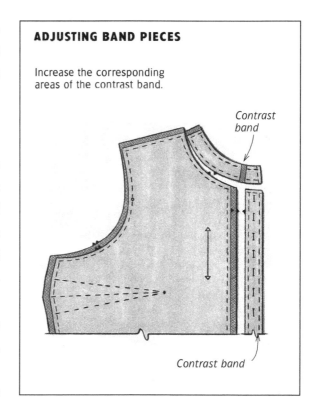

ADJUSTING BAND PIECES

Increase the corresponding areas of the contrast band.

Contrast band

Contrast band

BASIC SIZE ADJUSTMENTS IN LENGTH

	ACTUAL BODY MEASUREMENT	PATTERN MEASUREMENT	DIFFERENCE (+ OR −) = *MINIMUM* PATTERN ADJUSTMENT*
Back Waist Length			
Front Waist Length			
Sleeve Length (shoulder seam mark at top of cap to hem)			
Skirt Length (waist to hem)			
Pants Outseam (waist to hem)			
Crotch Seam Length			

*You must also add wearing and designer ease, as described on p. 72.

We all carry our height on different areas of our body. Usually, our proportions differ from those of a standardized dress form, so you need to adjust the pattern accordingly. Here, excess length is folded out, keeping the adjustment lines parallel.

Adjustments in Length" on the facing page to help determine the adjustments that are necessary for you.

To reduce length, fold out the excess as a pleat at the pattern adjustment line (see the photo on the facing page). To increase length, cut through the line, place strips of tissue, pattern drafting paper, or adding machine tape underneath the pattern, and tape it to the underlay at the needed increase (see the top photo below). (This is what is referred to as "slash and spread.") Be sure that all increases

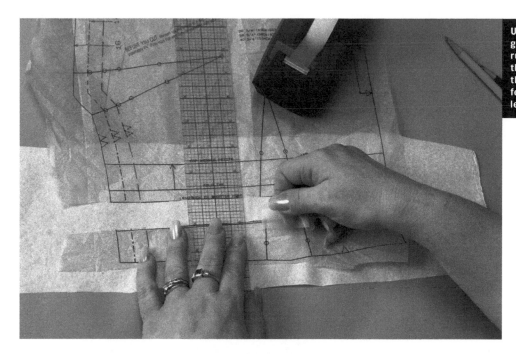

Use the crosswise grids on a clear ruler to line up the cut edges of the pattern piece for accurate length increases.

Draw in a length adjustment line wherever you need it.

> **tip** *Always remember to adjust every connecting pattern piece, such as a front facing for a blouse, to match the length of the front in the same place and by the same amount. For the chemise with the front diagonal drape, for example, if you add waist length to the front, you must also add it to the front overdrape and to the back as well.*

and decreases are perfectly parallel across the width of the adjusted area. If your pattern does not have adjustment lines, use your 30/60 degree triangle, L-square, or T-square to draw a straight line at a 90 degree angle to the lengthwise grainline across the midriff area for bodices, the lower hip for pants and skirts, and the upper arm area for sleeves (see the bottom photo on p. 71).

■ UNDERSTANDING EASE

In addition to comparing your body measurements with the pattern's measurements, you need to consider the pattern's ease. Ease is simply extra width and/or length built into each garment piece for wiggle room. If a garment's length and width exactly matched your lengths and widths, the garment would be too tight and uncomfortable to wear and would look terrible in nonstretch fabrics.

Wearing ease is those extra inches you need for comfort and mobility. See the chart "Minimum Wearing Ease for Plus Sizes" on the facing page for the *minimum* number of inches you should allow over your actual measurements when adjusting your pattern.

Design ease, on the other hand, is extra width or length that forms the overall design of the garment. For example, a blouson-waisted dress may have 4 in. of extra length at the center front and back so that about 2 in. folds attractively over the waistline. A full-pleated or gathered skirt may have yards of design ease. If the

MINIMUM WEARING EASE FOR PLUS SIZES
(nonstretch fabrics, in inches)

BODY/GARMENT LOCATION (BODY DIMENSION + EASE = GARMENT DIMENSION)	BODICE, BLOUSE, DRESS, PANTS, SKIRT (FIRST LAYER)	JACKET (SECOND LAYER)	COAT (THIRD LAYER)
Width			
Neck (jewel neckline)	1	1½	2
Bust	3–4	4	6
Waist (pants, skirt)	1½–6 (depending on style of waistband)	4	6
Waist (dress)	1½	—	—
Full hip	4	6	6–8
Upper arm	2	3–4	4–6
Wrist	1	—	—
Thigh	2–4	—	—
Length			
Bodice front waist length	1	1	1
Bodice back waist length	1	1	1
Pants crotch length	2–6	—	—

"width at hips" notation on the pattern piece says "60 in.," for example, and your hip measurement is 58 in., you will be able to squeeze into the skirt but it will look horrible. Without the intended design ease, the gathers will pull diagonally at the waist instead of draping in attractive vertical folds (see the drawings on p. 74). Never fit out design ease. Always err on the side of extra ease to allow for comfort, mobility, and spread.

Working with pleats

For some designs, such as all-around pleats in skirts, you must make all sizing increases in terms of the width of each pleat repeat. For example, if you just increased width at the side seams on a skirt with pleats all around as you would for a straight skirt, there might not be enough fabric at the sides to make an extra complete pleat to maintain the wearing ease, design ease, and design lines of the skirt.

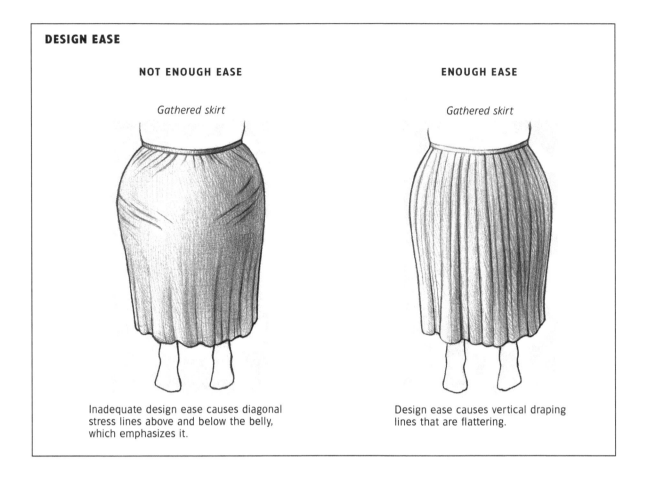

DESIGN EASE

NOT ENOUGH EASE

Gathered skirt

Inadequate design ease causes diagonal stress lines above and below the belly, which emphasizes it.

ENOUGH EASE

Gathered skirt

Design ease causes vertical draping lines that are flattering.

For a side-pleated skirt with 1-in. finished pleats, for example, the pleat width from the placement line on the top layer of fabric to the outer first fold might be 1 in.; from the first outer fold to the inner fold on the under-lap might be an additional 1 in. (although the width of the underlap is often less than the width of the finished pleat); and the width from the inner fold to the next place-ment line might be another 1 in., for a total pleat repeat of 3 in.

If you need to increase hip width, do so in multiples of that repeat. For example, if your hips are 1 in. wider than the measurement on the pattern envelope, the width of each repeat

might be 3 in. total, for a skirt with all-around 1-in. finished pleats. You need to add 3 in. to make one more complete pleat repeat and to maintain the 1-in. finished pleats and the over-all design of the skirt. In this case, you could slash and spread at the center back of the pat-tern, and increase 1½ in. at the center back foldline or seamline to fit your hips.

In a similar example, for a 2-in. hip width increase, however, you need to add two whole repeats, or 6 in. total width, by adding 1½ in. in width along the length of each side seam to make two more complete pleats at the sides. Always remember to measure your pattern from the first foldline of the pleat to the place-

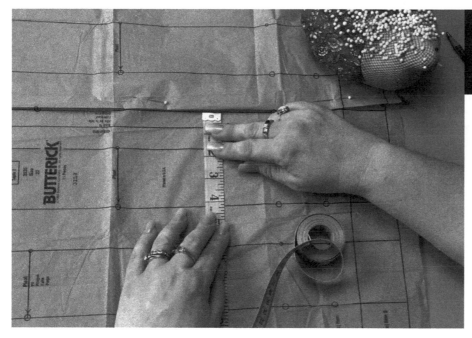

ADJUSTING PLEATS

Underlaps can be adjusted slightly as needed to fit and maintain design lines.

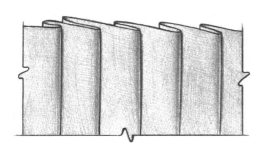

The distance between the first foldline of all pleats should be even.

ment line for the total width of a repeat, since the proportions of the parts of the pleat are not always even. Any extra width that may form at the waist and hips can be adjusted during the fitting process by tweaking the width of the underlaps, which don't show on the outside of the finished skirt (see the drawing above).

■ A NOTE ON PANTS

Adjust for width only at the side seams of pants. Do not mess with the center fronts and backs. Taper the width increases at the side seams to nothing at the knees, since most plus-sized legs are average sized below the knees. To check the crotch length, lay a tape measure on edge along the front and back crotch seamlines, and add the numbers together. Compare this total to your body measurement.

Always allow for wearing and design ease in the length of the crotch line. That four-point crotch seam juncture on finished pants should hang below the body at least 1 in. for flat front pants or stretch pants and as much as 4 in. for pants with front pleats or gathers. The goal is to allow the design ease of those pleats to drape attractively over the belly in flattering vertical lines, which also serves to distract viewers from the width of the hips.

Plus-sized women look best in European-cut pants, or ones with the crotch and inseam juncture positioned relatively forward on the body rather than toward the middle of the body. This prevents excess fabric from bunching up on the lower abdomen and allows more comfort for our backsides. Look for a pants pattern with a front crotch length that is obviously shorter than the back crotch length.

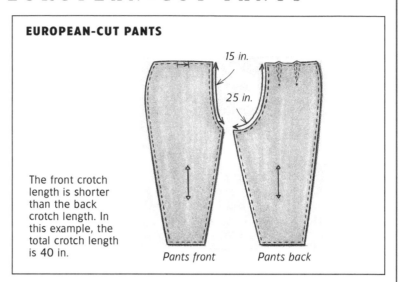

EUROPEAN-CUT PANTS

15 in.

25 in.

The front crotch length is shorter than the back crotch length. In this example, the total crotch length is 40 in.

Pants front   Pants back

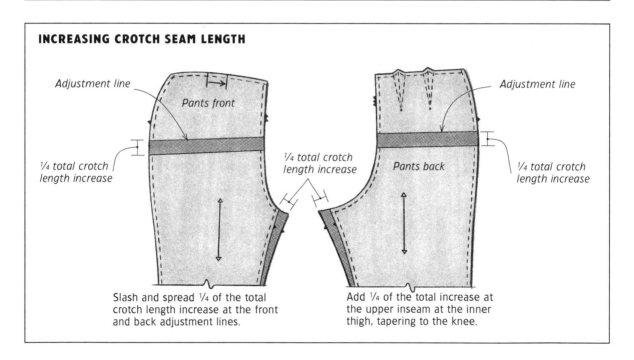

INCREASING CROTCH SEAM LENGTH

Adjustment line

Pants front

Adjustment line

¼ total crotch length increase

Pants back

¼ total crotch length increase

¼ total crotch length increase

Slash and spread ¼ of the total crotch length increase at the front and back adjustment lines.

Add ¼ of the total increase at the upper inseam at the inner thigh, tapering to the knee.

Plus-sized women can have very long crotch lengths; 40 in. or more is not uncommon for a size 30 or 32. To add length, slash and spread one-quarter of the total increase at the hipline on the front and back pieces (see the bottom drawings above). Then extend the front and back crotch cutting lines at the upper thigh the other one-quarter of the total increase. Connect this to the inner thigh cutting line, tapering to the knee.

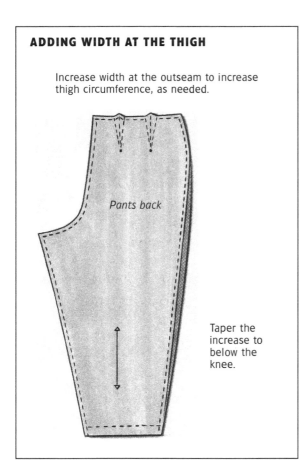
The width increases from the waist, which taper to the knee at the side seam, together with the increase in width from the extended crotch line, which tapers to the knee at the inseam, is usually plenty wide enough to accommodate the thigh circumference. Compare your thigh measurement with the pattern measurement for the front and back thigh and allow at least 2 in. of ease. If you need extra width, add it at the side seams and taper to just below the knees (see the drawing at left).

■ SAFETY FIRST

This simple method of sizing up a pattern usually results in a basted garment that is on the large side, meaning on the safe side. You can easily pin out excess fabric at seamlines when fitting, but you can't easily put it back after you've cut out the garment. Princess seams, particularly, need fitting over the chest area up to the shoulder, but this varies with each body.

Try not to be overwhelmed by all these possible adjustments. Most individuals only need to do a few of them, and you will normally make the same set of adjustments with every new pattern you use. With practice, you won't even have to cut tissue, tape it to seamlines, and mark the horizontal increases. I often just make notes to myself in red marker along the vertical seamlines so I remember to make adjustments by eye as I cut. While it might take you 10 to 30 minutes to size up a pattern to fit your body, that's less time than it takes to drive to the post office to return one catalog outfit that didn't fit!

adjusting the pattern to fit your figure variations

6

The basic width and length adjustments described in the last chapter will nearly always produce garment pieces in basically the right shape and size for you, but you may still need a few additional adjustments. That's because there are figure variations common to large women that are easily observed but not so easily measured. For example, just because a woman has a 46-in. bust and a chest measurement of 44 in., you can't assume she is a B cup size. If she has a broad and muscular back, she could be an A cup; if she has a relatively narrow waist, she might be a C or D cup size. Likewise, a 63-in. hip could describe a body with a fairly flat tummy and prominent backside, one with a large hanging belly and a relatively small fanny, someone who carries her weight on each side at the thighs with a fairly flat tummy and fanny, or someone who is evenly round all around.

Even elaborate measuring systems, such as ones that measure half or quarter arcs around the body to compile hundreds of measurements, cannot take the place of observation. This is because we take two-dimensional measurements on our three-dimensional bodies. With tape measure technology, it's impossible to map the size and location of every bump and curve on our unique figures. So remember, measurements tell you *how much,* but they do not tell you *where!*

If you did not need to make any of the adjustments described in the last chapter, you may still need to adjust for figure variations, particularly if your basic body measurements closely coincide with standardized pattern measurements. Some of these adjustments must be made before the garment is cut. Since the extra length and width produced in most of these adjustments can always be fitted out later, always err on the side of safety.

So take a long look in the mirror, and analyze how your unique bumps and curves vary from those of a standardized dress form. For example, is your bust smaller or larger than average? Are the apexes wider apart or lower than average? Do you have a rounded upper back, large upper arms, or a big belly? Then follow the instructions for your specific figure variations that I give in this chapter.

You will probably notice that I will often instruct you to adjust a pattern piece by an unspecified amount. Sewing is at least as much an art as it is a science. Even when I have specified a measurement, please understand that it is only a guideline. Measurements, no matter how elaborate, can't tell you exactly *where* on a garment you need to position width and length adequately for your unique body shape. The goal of all pattern adjustments as described in the previous chapter and this one is to correct and prevent any problems that cannot be cured during a basted fitting. Be assured that nearly all other fitting adjustments can be completed at that time, as long as you have plenty of width and length to work with.

■ BUST ADJUSTMENTS

Nearly all commercial patterns are drafted for a B cup size, and most patternmakers assume that your bust is as perky at age 60 as it was at age 20. Of course, we know better. The shape, size, and position of our bust varies greatly from woman to woman, and it also varies during an individual's lifetime.

Darts

If you hold a yard of muslin across your chest and look in the mirror, you will see that two vertical folds of fabric form naturally from the bust apexes to the lower edge of the fabric (see the photo on the facing page). These folds are actually darts, whether they are stitched down as triangular or diamond-shaped darts or take the form of dart equivalents, such as tucks, gathers, seams, or other design features. The depth of the fold is called the dart's *take-up,* and that depth varies with the wearer's cup size, the number of darts that take up the extra fabric above and below the larger circumference of the bustline, and the position of those darts.

Just as all circles are round, all garments have darts, whether you know it or not. Note the vertical folds that naturally form below the bust apexes.

Many plus-sized commercial patterns are loose and shapeless. You can add darts for a more sophisticated fit and more attractive design lines. You can also enlarge darts to accommodate cup sizes greater than a B; you can divide them from one large dart to two or more smaller ones; you can rotate them to different areas of a bodice; and you can hide them in design features such as geometric and princess seams.

FINDING YOUR CORRECT APEX POSITION Before you get to play with darts, you have to calculate their correct position. Bust darts should point to the bust apexes. Often, the position of the apex mark on the pattern and the location of your bust are not the same.

Remember your high school geometry? Now you get to use it! Compare the measurements that you recorded on p. 59 for side neck to apex, apex to apex, and apex to center front at waist to those on the pattern to triangulate your bust. The point at which these three lines intersect is your apex position. If necessary, you can guess at the side neck position for designs with scooped necklines. After you have marked your apex position on the pattern, connect the corrected apex mark to the original sides of the dart angle. To avoid that 50s pointy look, measure about 1 in. down the dart's centerline from the apex mark to locate the vertex of the new dart angle, and redraw the completed dart (see the drawings on p. 82).

ADDING A DART Now that you know where your correct apex position is on the pattern, you can draft darts on shapeless bodices for a more sophisticated fit. For a side or underarm dart, follow these steps.

1. Draw a line from the corrected apex mark to the side seam below the underarm.

2. Then draw a line at a right angle to the waist up vertically to the apex, pivoting at the apex and continuing just to but not through the armscye notch (see the photo on p. 82). Use small pieces of transparent tape over

FINDING THE CORRECT BUST APEX POSITION

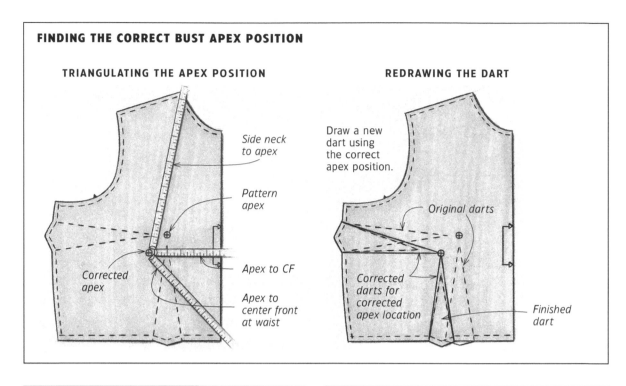

TRIANGULATING THE APEX POSITION

Side neck to apex

Pattern apex

Corrected apex

Apex to CF

Apex to center front at waist

REDRAWING THE DART

Draw a new dart using the correct apex position.

Original darts

Corrected darts for corrected apex location

Finished dart

The three adjustment lines are drawn using your corrected apex mark. There is one from the side seam to the apex, one from the waist to the apex, and finally one from the apex to the armscye notch.

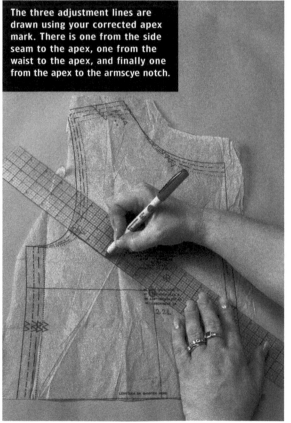

NOTE

Standard pattern drafting guidelines are based on small sizes, so they may not be adequate for plus sizes. A C cup on a size 8 woman, after all, does not look like a C cup on a size 32. Use these numbers as guidelines only, and err on the side of extra spread if in doubt. For each additional cup size larger than a DD, spread about 1 in.

the armscye notch and apex mark for reinforcement.

3. Cut along the vertical line, pivoting through the apex, just to but not through the notch.

4. Cut the horizontal underarm line just to but not through the apex mark.

5. As shown in the left photo on the facing page, spread the pattern along the vertical line

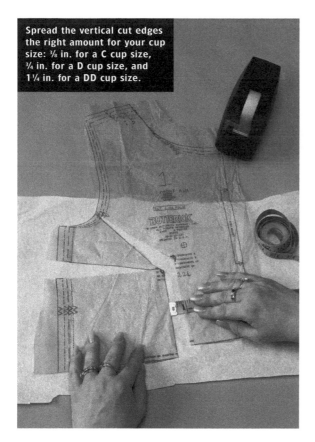

Spread the vertical cut edges the right amount for your cup size: ⅜ in. for a C cup size, ¾ in. for a D cup size, and 1¼ in. for a DD cup size.

Lengthen the center front so it is level with the bottom of the pattern piece. Then draw in the new darts.

from waist to apex to a width of ⅜ in. for a C cup, ¾ in. for a D cup, and 1¼ in. for a DD cup.

6. As you spread the vertical cut, the new underarm dart will automatically open up the correct amount.

7. Tape the pattern to a tissue underlay as you adjust it.

8. Draw in the legs for the new underarm dart from the newly formed space at the side seam to the vertex, about 1 in. from the bust apex.

9. Last, extend the center front line to the waistline seam or hem area (see the right photo above). The increased width at the vertical slash can be left as design ease for a looser fit at the waist area, or it can be taken out as a vertical dart or other design feature.

For a vertical dart, reposition the dart if necessary to keep it centered below the corrected apex and at right angles to the waistline, especially if you have adjusted width at the bust and waist.

ROTATING AND DIVIDING DARTS Instead of one very large dart to accommodate the increase in width and length over your bustline, you can distribute some of the depth of that dart to other areas of a bodice in the form of one or more additional darts, especially if you are large busted. In fact, darts can be rotated all around the apex of the bust for different design effects. Follow these steps to rotate a dart.

1. Start by reinforcing the corrected apex mark with a small piece of transparent tape.

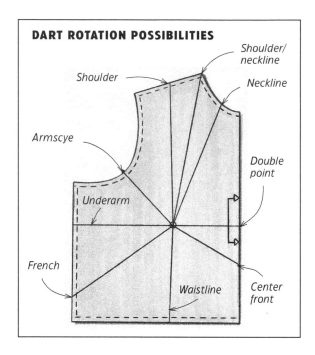

DART ROTATION POSSIBILITIES

Shoulder

Shoulder/neckline

Neckline

Armscye

Double point

Underarm

French

Waistline

Center front

tip *While all darts enhance the fit of garments and add interesting design detail, plus-sized women may find that vertical darts, French darts (which run diagonally from the side seam at the waist up to the bust), and underarm darts are most flattering.*

2. Draw new dart sides from the base of the original dart to the corrected apex. Then cut out the area of the entire dart take-up.

3. Draw a new line for an additional dart wherever you would like to position it (see the drawing above); cut this line just to but not through the apex mark.

4. Close the original dart, and like magic, the new dart will open to the correct depth.

5. Back up the vertex about 1 in. as usual, and redraw the completed dart.

6. Last, fold the pattern tissue at the new dart's foldline as you will your garment, and draw a new cutting line for the side seam at the base of the dart (see the top left drawing on the facing page). This is called "truing."

To divide a dart and redistribute its depth and width to two or more darts, follow steps 1 through 3, and draw as many dart lines as you want for your design. Then follow the same procedure for rotating, but instead of closing the original dart, just leave it open so that the depth of each dart is equal (see the top right drawing on the facing page). You can also close the original dart and open up any number of new ones. Then complete the adjustment by following steps 5 and 6.

Adjusting princess seams for cup size

A princess seam is actually a dart in disguise and is an example of a dart equivalent. If you line up a princess-seamed bodice front and side front at the apex, you will see that it's just like a basic bodice with a shoulder dart and a waist dart. Like all bust darts, if your bust is larger than a B cup, you must also adjust princess seams to fit your cup size.

There are two ways to achieve this adjustment. For the first method, follow these steps.

1. Triangulate your apex position on the bodice front just as you did for a dart-fitted bodice (see p. 82). You may need to shift the princess seam right or left on the front and side front pattern pieces to center the seam over your apex position so that the curves of the seam can accommodate the curves of your bust.

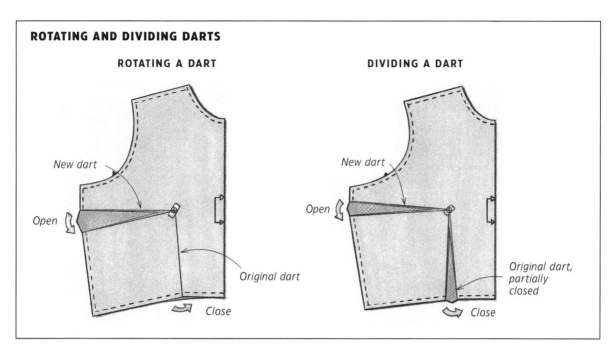

ROTATING AND DIVIDING DARTS

ROTATING A DART

New dart

Open

Original dart

Close

DIVIDING A DART

New dart

Open

Original dart, partially closed

Close

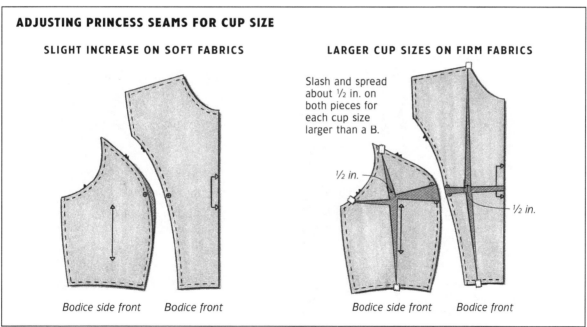

ADJUSTING PRINCESS SEAMS FOR CUP SIZE

SLIGHT INCREASE ON SOFT FABRICS

Bodice side front   Bodice front

LARGER CUP SIZES ON FIRM FABRICS

Slash and spread about ½ in. on both pieces for each cup size larger than a B.

½ in.

½ in.

Bodice side front   Bodice front

2. If the increase is fairly small, say to a C cup, and the fabric is soft, loosely woven, and easy to ease, you can simply extend the curve of the side front at the apex very slightly and ease the added length into the front near the apex as you sew the princess seam (see the bottom left drawing above). This method results in a gently curved princess seam that skims the figure.

3. For stiffer or thicker fabrics and cup sizes larger than a C, you must draft enough length

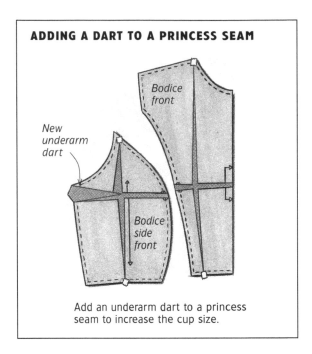

ADDING A DART TO A PRINCESS SEAM

Bodice front

New underarm dart

Bodice side front

Add an underarm dart to a princess seam to increase the cup size.

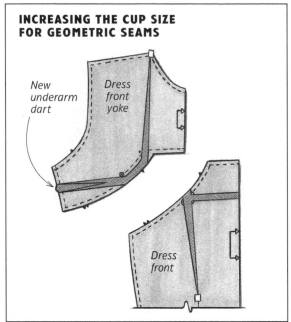

INCREASING THE CUP SIZE FOR GEOMETRIC SEAMS

New underarm dart

Dress front yoke

Dress front

and width to accommodate your increased cup size. Slash the front and side front pattern pieces horizontally at the apex mark just to but not through the side seam.

4. Then slash the pattern vertically from the waist just to but not through the side neck area.

5. Spread the slashes on both pattern pieces in both directions approximately ½ in. per cup size larger than a B, and redraw the cutting lines (see the bottom right drawing on p. 85). Note that this is an ample amount of spread that can be easily pinned out at the princess seamlines during a fitting, if needed.

Alternately, you can add a dart to a princess seam for easier sewing of stiff fabrics like duchesse satin and for a close and precise fit on D cups or larger. Follow these steps.

1. Triangulate your apex position on the bodice front just as you did for a dart-fitted bodice (see p. 82). You may need to shift the

princess seam right or left on the front and side front pattern pieces to center the seam over your apex position so the curves of the seam can accommodate the curves of your bust.

2. Slash and spread as above, only cut through the pattern horizontally at the side seam.

3. Spread at the side seam also, and then draw a new underarm dart to within 1 in. of the bust apex on the princess seam to take up the added length of the side seam (see the left drawing above). The new dart is hardly noticeable under the arm, but when sewn, it nicely accommodates the fullness of the side of the bust.

Darts are often hidden in design features such as geometric seams, yokes, gathers, tucks, and so on. As for princess seams, you need to slash and spread at the correct bust apex for larger cup sizes as above, remembering to adjust any corresponding pattern pieces (see the right drawing above). As always, it is best to err on

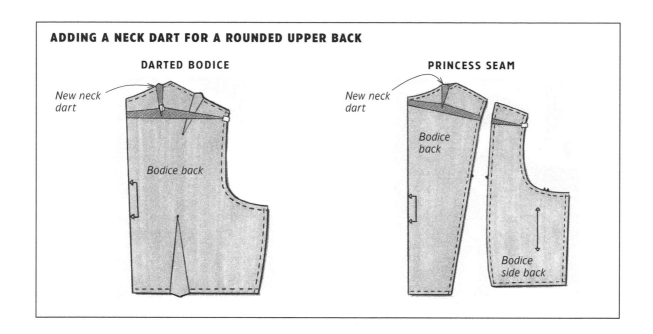

ADDING A NECK DART FOR A ROUNDED UPPER BACK

DARTED BODICE

New neck dart

Bodice back

PRINCESS SEAM

New neck dart

Bodice back

Bodice side back

the side of extra length and width over the bust, since extra fabric can be pinned out during the fitting process later.

ROUNDED UPPER BACK

Most plus-sized women have a rounded upper back, also called a dowager's hump or tailor's hump. To accommodate it, you need to add extra length and width, especially if you have not already done so. Simply slash the pattern horizontally from the center back to the end of the shoulder seam and vertically from the neck seam to the first adjustment line (see the drawings above). Add a neckline dart to snug the upper bodice to your neck area. You can adjust the length of this new dart to accommodate your upper back curves during a fitting later.

LARGE UPPER ARMS

Average-sized women usually have upper arms shaped like the business end of a baseball bat, but many plus-sized womens' upper arms are shaped more like footballs. Because our arms are more spherical than cylindrical, they need extra length and width in the upper arm. If you need additional ease and you did not adjust this area as described in the last chapter because your bust measurement closely corresponds to the pattern's standardized measurement, adjust the pattern as follows.

1. Slash vertically from the shoulder mark on the top of the sleeve cap toward the hem; slash horizontally from one sleeve seam to the other.

2. Spread the desired increase horizontally, and allow the vertical slashes to overlap. Tape to an underlay (see the top drawing on p. 88).

3. For the extra length you need, redraw the sleeve cap as described on p. 67.

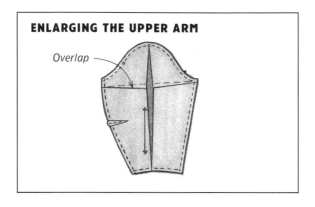

ENLARGING THE UPPER ARM

Overlap

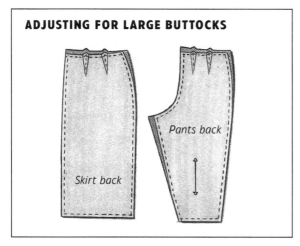

ADJUSTING FOR LARGE BUTTOCKS

Skirt back

Pants back

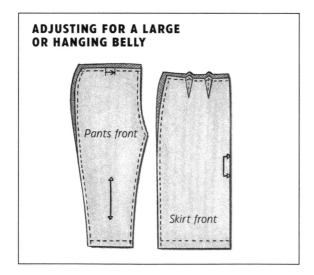

**ADJUSTING FOR A LARGE
OR HANGING BELLY**

Pants front

Skirt front

■ LARGE BUTTOCKS

Even if your hip and waist measurements closely correspond to the pattern's and you have a small tummy, you may need to adjust for a large or prominent backside. As usual, you need to add length and width. For pants, raise the waistline a couple of inches from center back tapering to the side seams, and lengthen the back crotch line an equal amount by extending it at the inseam, tapering to the knee. Adjust skirts by raising the back waist seam in the same manner and adding width at the side seam. Any excess adjustment can be corrected at the first fitting.

■ LARGE OR HANGING BELLY

This adjustment is exactly the same as for a large backside, only you do it on the front pattern piece. Raise the waistline of skirts and pants from center front tapering to the side seams, and add width at the hips so the garment flows over your tummy and does not cling to it. For pants, increase the length of the front crotch seam the same amount you added at the center front to maintain adequate crotch seam length.

■ LARGE NECK

If you haven't adjusted the jewel neck length at the shoulder seams, just scoop the neckline lower and wider for comfort, as described on p. 66. Remember to also adjust or redraft all corresponding pattern pieces, such as facings, yokes, or collars.

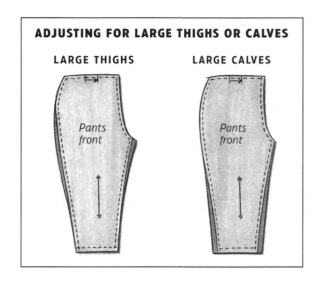

ADJUSTING FOR LARGE THIGHS OR CALVES

LARGE THIGHS

LARGE CALVES

Pants front

Pants front

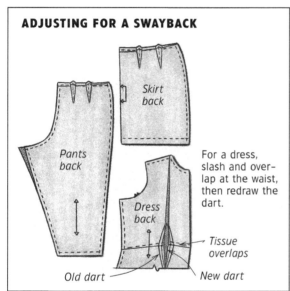

ADJUSTING FOR A SWAYBACK

Skirt back

Pants back

Dress back

For a dress, slash and overlap at the waist, then redraw the dart.

Old dart

Tissue overlaps

New dart

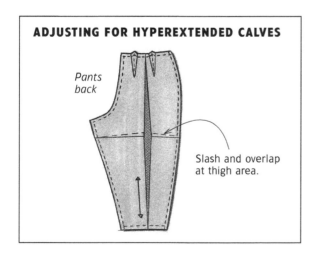

ADJUSTING FOR HYPEREXTENDED CALVES

Pants back

Slash and overlap at thigh area.

■ LARGE LEGS

For very large thighs or calves, widen at the side seams in the thigh area, tapering to the knee. Also for calves, you can flair the pants leg at the inseam and outseam for additional width.

■ SWAYBACK

If you have a swayback, the small of your back is more concave than it is for average figures, so you need less fabric to skim this area. You may need to shorten the length of the center back area near the waist for skirts, dresses, and pants. If your buttocks are not unusually large, just lower the waistline slightly at center back, tapering to the side seams for skirts and pants. Pleat out a small length decrease on dresses at the waist center back, leaving the side seams intact. On pants, when you lower the waistline at center back, you also shorten the crotch length, so add the same amount at the pants back inseam to compensate.

■ HYPEREXTENDED CALVES

If you have a swayback and a big belly, you may stand with your knees locked and your calf muscles flexed toward the back for balance. On pants, this can cause extra fabric to drape in horizontal folds between the buttocks and the calves. Too much length between the widest part of the buttocks curve and the greatest extension of the back of the calves causes this. After adjusting for swayback, pleat out a small bit of length on the pants back pattern piece below the crotch line by slashing vertically, then horizontally, to but not through the side seam and inseam, and overlapping the cut edges.

design modifications for plus sizes

■ ■ **7** ■

Once you have your pattern adjusted to fit your body size and your figure variations, there are changes you may wish to add to your plus-sized designs to make them more comfortable, durable, and attractive.

■ WAISTBANDS

Standard waistbands do not work well for plus sizes. When you sit or bend over, they feel constrictive as soft body tissues shift and compress, and they tend to roll over no matter how stiffly they are interfaced. Luckily, it's easy to sew a more comfortable and attractive waistband. Select the band style that is best for your garment design and fabric and for your comfort.

> **tip** *As you follow the instructions for all these waistband variations, bear in mind that there is no need to transfer pattern marks from the original band to your adjusted band because you are going to cut the waistband to fit the waist of your pants or skirt. It is, after all, just a long, skinny rectangle.*

All-elastic waistbands

All-elastic waistbands are wonderful for casual, pull-on pants and skirts constructed from thin, soft, and drapey fabrics, such as sueded silk or rayon, challis, or even lightweight wool crepe. They are also appropriate for pants or skirts designed to be worn with an overblouse or tunic.

To substitute an elastic band for a standard one, you first need to adjust the skirt or pants so that the waist is about as wide as the hips, so you can pull the garment on easily. Here's how.

1. Widen the side seam from the full hip to the waist, ignore all the darts or tucks on the front piece, and do not sew up the outer set of darts on the back piece. I like to retain the inner set of darts on the back to reduce bulk over the center area of the fanny and to give the garment a smoother appearance.

2. Measure the width of the adjusted waist seam, excluding seam allowances and the take-up of any remaining darts on the pattern back.

3. Cut the new waistband the length of the garment's waist plus 1¼ in. for seam allowances

APPRAISE YOUR PATTERN'S WAISTBAND

Please avoid patterns without a separate waistband, unless you are making pajama bottoms. These cut-on bands simply fold over at the top of the garment and are topstitched to form an elastic casing. They do not allow even distribution of ease around the body as elastic in a sewn-on casing does. If you have one of these patterns, just trim off the extension for the elastic casing evenly, leaving a seam allowance at the waist mark. Discard the trimmed-off piece, and construct the garment as if it had a sewn-on band.

Also, a pattern that calls for a waistband with only one wide piece of elastic produces a band that looks bulky and unrefined and is suitable only when it is covered by an overblouse. Likewise, elastic that is stitched directly to the band or the garment's waist distributes ease around the body only where you sew it. Elastics inside casings, on the other hand, can distribute ease all around the body anywhere you need it, so they are more comfortable and more attractive.

MAKING A SEPARATE WAISTBAND PIECE

Cutting line

Casing foldline

Waist mark

Pants front

Trim off a cut-on waistband, leaving a seam allowance above the waist mark.

ADJUSTING A PATTERN FOR AN ELASTIC WAISTBAND

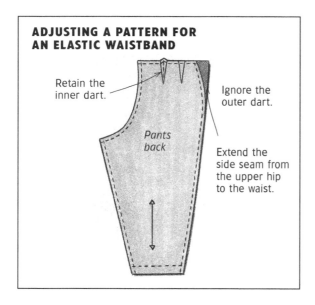

Retain the inner dart.

Ignore the outer dart.

Extend the side seam from the upper hip to the waist.

Pants back

MEASURING FOR THE NEW WAISTBAND

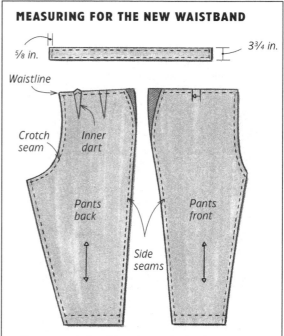

⅝ in.

3¾ in.

Waistline

Crotch seam

Inner dart

Pants back

Pants front

Side seams

The new waistband length equals the distance from the crotch seam to the inner dart edge *plus* the inner dart edge to the side seam line (pants back) and the distance from the front side seam to the crotch seam (pants front) *plus* seam allowances.

(⅝ in. at each end) by 3¾ in. wide for a 1¼-in.-wide finished band. Cutting the band along a selvage makes measuring and cutting faster.

4. Sew the ends of the band with right sides together; trim, and press open the seam allowance.

5. Fold this circular band in half lengthwise with wrong sides together, and press it.

6. Baste the long seam allowances of the band together just inside the seamline.

7. Sew the band to the garment waist, placing the band seam at center back (which will help you remember how to wear the garment).

8. Trim and finish the waist seam by serging, zigzagging, or applying a very lightweight binding. Press the seam down.

9. To help prevent the band from rolling, edgestitch the upper edge of the band.

10. Decide if you want to use two ½-in. pieces of elastic, which are better for medium-weight fabrics, or three ¼-in. elastics, which are better for lightweight fabrics. Sew the appropriate

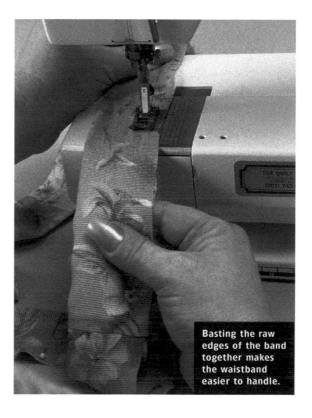

Basting the raw edges of the band together makes the waistband easier to handle.

number of evenly spaced channels. Don't be overly worried if your stitching wobbles slightly because it won't show on the finished band as long as all of the channels are wide enough to accommodate the size of elastic you have chosen.

11. Use a seam ripper to open up the center back band seam carefully on the inside of the garment only, and only between the stitching lines for the channels.

12. While standing, stretch two or three lengths of elastic snugly but comfortably around your waist, and add 1 in. to that length for an overlap. Cut the pieces of elastic to length.

13. Insert the elastics all at once into the casings by attaching the ends to safety pins and shoving them along inside the casings, taking care to pin the far ends when they are about 2 in. from the casing openings to secure them temporarily.

14. Overlap each set of ends by ½ in., and bartack twice to secure.

15. Finally, grab the waistband on each side and stretch it out fully a few times, which will distribute the ease evenly along the band and pop the elastics back inside the casing openings.

16. Slipstitch the openings closed, if desired.

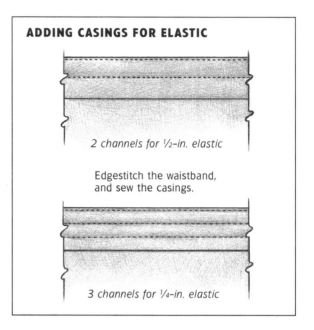

ADDING CASINGS FOR ELASTIC

2 channels for ½-in. elastic

Edgestitch the waistband, and sew the casings.

3 channels for ¼-in. elastic

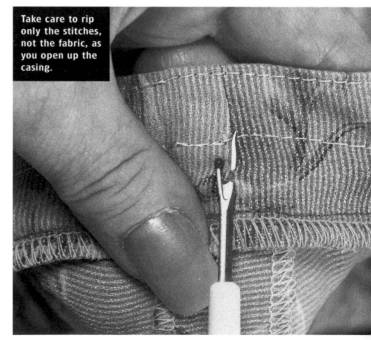

Take care to rip only the stitches, not the fabric, as you open up the casing.

> **tip** *Do not follow the old "waist measurement plus 1 in." rule for cutting elastic, or your pants will fall down. Every piece of elastic and every combination of multiple elastics will vary in stretchiness and the ability to support the weight of a garment; heavier garments, for example, necessitate less stretch to avoid drooping.*

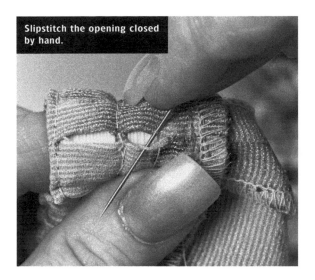

Slipstitch the opening closed by hand.

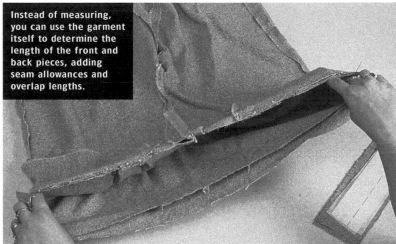

Instead of measuring, you can use the garment itself to determine the length of the front and back pieces, adding seam allowances and overlap lengths.

Partial elastic waistbands

For a more tailored look, which is also suitable for heavier fabrics, you can combine a standard and an elastic waistband. There are a number of variations on this theme. Which style of band you choose depends on the style of garment and its intended use. For example, for a business suit worn with the jacket open, a side-elastic band looks neat and tailored at the center front. For sporty pants, a back elastic band allows for plenty of comfort and movement but reduces bulk over the front waist area.

BACK ELASTIC WAISTBAND FOR FLY-FRONT GARMENTS

Use a back elastic waistband on fly-front pants and skirts. Start by adjusting the pants or skirt width on the back pattern piece from waist to hip, and retain only the inside back darts (see p. 93).

For fly-front pants and skirts, use the following method.

1. Cut three waistband pieces, one to fit the adjusted back pattern piece and two to fit each side of the constructed front piece of the garment, adding seam allowances and a 2⅝-in. underlap for the front left-side band.

2. Apply waistband interfacing to the front two pieces only; then sew the three pieces together at the side seams, trim, and press the seams open.

3. Fold the band lengthwise at the interfacing foldlines, and press the entire band (see the top photo on p. 96).

4. Finish one long edge of the inside of the band, usually the edge with the wider waistband interfacing.

5. Sew the unfinished edge of the band to the garment waist with right sides together and with the band up, just outside the interfacing and 1¼ in. from the fold, matching at the side seams. Trim and grade the waist seam.

6. Finish the right end of the band even with the fly overlap by folding the band lengthwise with right sides together and stitching the end of the band. Trim and grade the seam, and turn the band right side out.

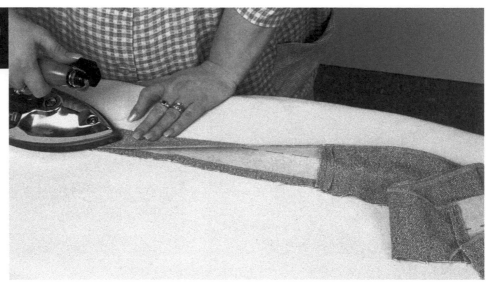

It's easier to press the fold of the band before it is sewn to the garment.

At the band ends, fold the band right sides together. For the overlap, stitch the end only so it will be even with the opening edge of the fly. For the underlap shown here, sew the end, pivot, and sew the waist edges only to the zipper.

For the left band, fold the band lengthwise with right sides together, sew the end of the band 2 in. from the left zipper edge, pivot at the corner, and continue stitching to the zipper. Trim and grade the seam, then turn the underlap end of the band right side out.

7. Pin the finished edge of the folded back waistband over the seam allowance from side seam to side seam, on the right side of the band, ensuring that the seam allowance is pushed up into the folded band.

8. From the right side, stitch in the ditch with a short stitch length from side seam to side seam on the band back only to secure it. Note that the front band will be secured after the elastic is inserted.

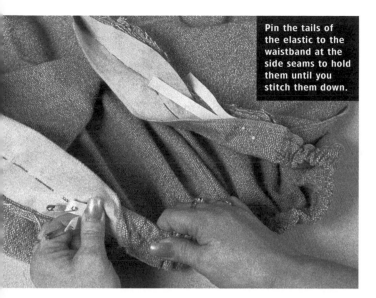

Pin the tails of the elastic to the waistband at the side seams to hold them until you stitch them down.

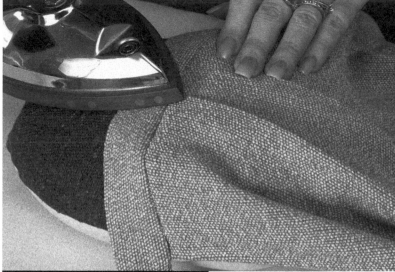

Press the finished band over a tailor's ham to shape it to your waist's contours. Note that the ditch stitching, even in bright pink thread, is hardly visible on the completed band. (For clarity, a press cloth was not used.)

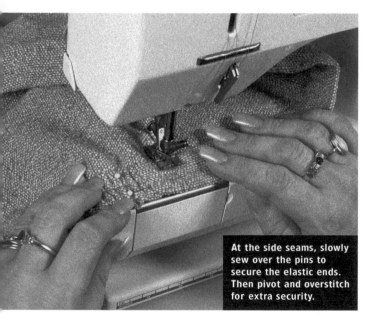

At the side seams, slowly sew over the pins to secure the elastic ends. Then pivot and overstitch for extra security.

9. Then edgestitch the upper edge of the back band, sew channels, and insert elastic as for an all-elastic waistband (see steps 10 through 13 on pp. 93-94); instead of bar-tacking the ends of the elastics, secure them at each side seam with pins.

10. To complete the band, pin the band fronts and stitch in the ditch as above, pivoting at the side seams to stitch in the side seam ditch in order to secure the elastics. Turn your work 180 degrees, and stitch in the side seam ditch once more for extra security.

11. Top-press the waistband fronts with a pressing cloth over a ham, moving the iron from the top of the band toward the bottom to shift the fabric very slightly over the waist seamline and cover the ditch stitching.

Back-elastic, pull-on waistband

You can sew a back elastic, pull-on band for skirts or pants the same way as you did the waistband for fly-front pants. Sew up the front darts or tucks before you measure the front and back band lengths. Interface the front band only, sew the front and back bands together at the side seams, and ignore the steps to complete the band ends.

Side-elastic waistband

A side-elastic waistband is another variation on this theme. The elastic inserts run from back dart to front dart or tuck, so it hardly shows when your arms are down or you wear a jacket. Construct one following these steps.

1. As for all elastic waistbands, adjust the pattern front and back by ignoring the outside set of darts or tucks, retaining the inner set, and widening the waist to about the same width as the full hip.

2. To calculate the length of the waistband, measure the total new waist length on the pattern, excluding seam allowances and any retained dart or tuck take-ups; or measure the garment when you are ready to sew the waistband.

3. Mark the location of the center front, center back, and any retained darts or tucks on the waistband by holding the waistband and garment waist seams together as if you were ready to sew them.

4. Interface the band at center front and center back between the tucks or darts only.

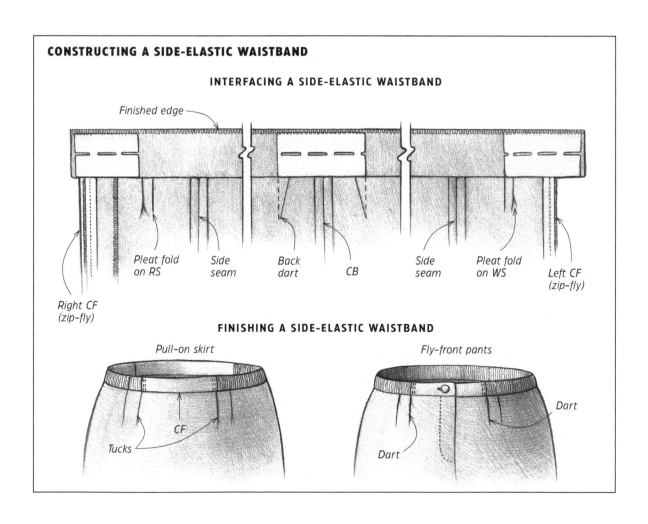

CONSTRUCTING A SIDE-ELASTIC WAISTBAND

INTERFACING A SIDE-ELASTIC WAISTBAND

Finished edge

Right CF (zip-fly)
Pleat fold on RS
Side seam
Back dart
CB
Side seam
Pleat fold on WS
Left CF (zip-fly)

FINISHING A SIDE-ELASTIC WAISTBAND

Pull-on skirt
Tucks
CF

Fly-front pants
Dart
Dart

5. Attach the band to the pants or skirt as for a back-elastic waistband.

6. Stitch in the ditch to secure the waistband in the side areas first between the darts or tucks; then edgestitch and sew the channels as usual in the side areas only.

7. Insert the elastic, and pin to secure.

8. Finish the band ends, if appropriate, and stitch in the ditch of the interfaced waistband areas, pivoting across the elastic ends twice to secure them.

Tailored elastic waistband

A tailored elastic waistband provides a little bit of stretch but gives the more tailored appearance of a conventional waistband. It's great for pants and skirts made of bulky knits, such as wool double-knits, or for apple-shaped women whose hips are not much wider than their waists. To make this waistband, either you must have a zippered opening or the fabric must stretch enough or be wide enough for you to pull the new waist width over your hips. Follow these steps.

1. Start by adjusting the pattern front and back at the upper side seams only by about 1 in. at each side seam edge, for an extra 4 in. of width all together (see the drawings on p. 100).

2. Cut a waistband the same way as for the other elastic waistband methods. For zippered openings, apply interfacing to the last 1 in. of the overlap and the last 3 in. of the underlap.

3. For pull-on bands, sew the center back seam, and finish the long underside edge of the band. Then press the band lengthwise as usual.

4. Cut 1-in.-wide elastic, preferably the ribbed, nonroll variety, to fit snugly around your waist. For pull-on garments, lap the elastic ends, and bar-tack to secure.

5. Fold the elastic to mark it in quarters. Next, open up the fold of the band as you would with a standard waistband, and pin the long unfinished edge to the garment waist with right sides together. Sew, trim, and grade the seam.

6. With the pants or skirt up and the unfolded waistband down, pin the quarter marks on the elastic to the waistband seam allowance only, at center front, center back, and the side seams.

7. For pull-on garments, sew the edge of the elastic with a zigzag to the waist seam allowance only, all around the waistband circle. For zippered garments, start about 1 in. from the overlap end and 3 in. from the underlap, keeping the elastic edge close to the waistband seamline (see the drawings on p. 100). Stretch the elastic slightly between the quarter marks to distribute the ease evenly as you sew it to the seam allowance.

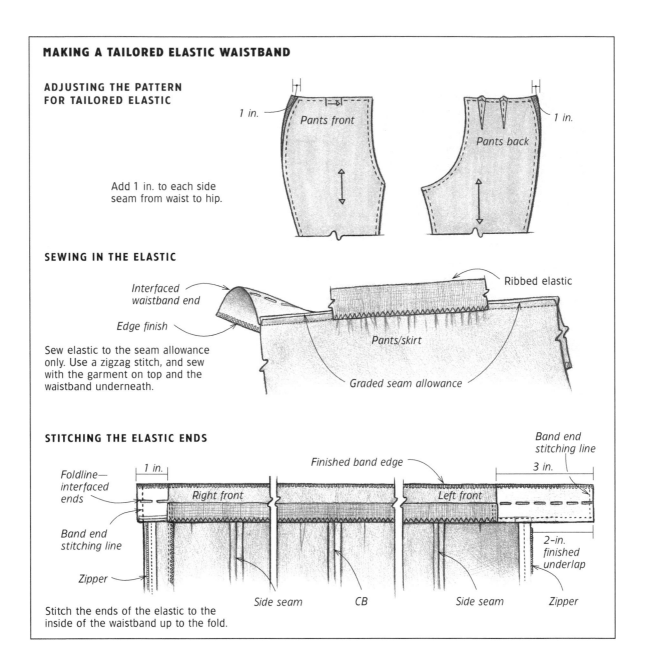

MAKING A TAILORED ELASTIC WAISTBAND

ADJUSTING THE PATTERN FOR TAILORED ELASTIC

Add 1 in. to each side seam from waist to hip.

1 in.

Pants front

Pants back

1 in.

SEWING IN THE ELASTIC

Interfaced waistband end

Edge finish

Sew elastic to the seam allowance only. Use a zigzag stitch, and sew with the garment on top and the waistband underneath.

Ribbed elastic

Pants/skirt

Graded seam allowance

STITCHING THE ELASTIC ENDS

Foldline—interfaced ends

1 in.

Finished band edge

Band end stitching line

3 in.

Right front

Left front

Band end stitching line

Zipper

2-in. finished underlap

Side seam   CB   Side seam   *Zipper*

Stitch the ends of the elastic to the inside of the waistband up to the fold.

---

8. Fold the waistband and the elastic up and stitch the elastic ends on zippered garments to the inside of the waistband, just up to the fold. **9.** Finish the ends of the band, if appropriate, then fold the band down, and stitch in the waistband seam ditch to finish, stretching slightly as you sew.

Grosgrain ribbon facing

This method is faster than a facing and can be a godsend when you are too short on fabric to cut a waistband. It's especially nice for zippered garments made of bulky wovens like tweeds and for women with short torsos. This waist finish can be applied with or without elastic sides. For side elastic, construct the garment as for the other elastic waistbands, converting the outside darts or pleats to ease and adding additional width to the upper side seams. To make a ribbon facing, follow these steps.

1. Measure a piece of 7/8-in. grosgrain ribbon the length of the waistline seam plus 1 in. If you can find it, cotton/acetate grosgrain ribbon, sometimes called petersham, is better than polyester ribbon. It will take a press so you can shape it, and it softens with age and will stretch slightly to conform to your curves.

2. Use your steam iron to stretch the ribbon into a curved shape; let the ribbon cool and dry.

3. With the right side of the garment up, edgestitch the inner, shorter curve of the ribbon to the garment just inside the waist seamline, folding the ends under at the openings.

4. Then turn the ribbon down to the wrong side of the garment, and top-press the waist with a press cloth over a tailor's ham to shape it.

5. For a nonelastic waist, tack the lower edge of the ribbon to the darts, seam allowances, and zipper tape. For a side-elastic finish, stitch

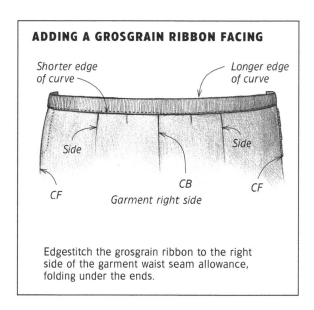

ADDING A GROSGRAIN RIBBON FACING

Shorter edge of curve

Longer edge of curve

Side

Side

CF

CB

CF

Garment right side

Edgestitch the grosgrain ribbon to the right side of the garment waist seam allowance, folding under the ends.

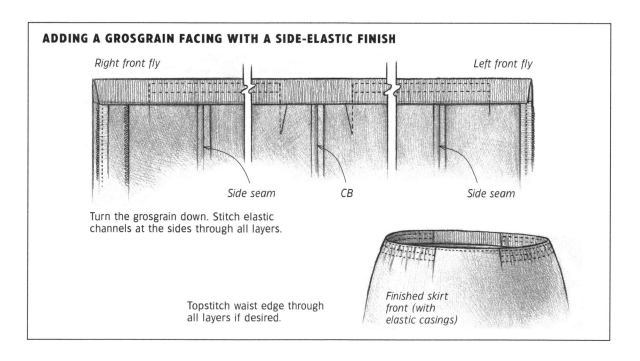

ADDING A GROSGRAIN FACING WITH A SIDE-ELASTIC FINISH

Right front fly

Left front fly

Side seam

CB

Side seam

Turn the grosgrain down. Stitch elastic channels at the sides through all layers.

Topstitch waist edge through all layers if desired.

Finished skirt front (with elastic casings)

down the lower edge of the ribbon to the garment in the side areas as for the side-elastic waistband, sew channels if desired, insert the elastic, and sew through all layers to secure the ends (see the bottom drawings on p. 101). Topstitch near the skirt waist edge through all layers, if desired.

Double fasteners for waistbands

Plus-sized waistbands typically endure more stress as we move and sit than do average bands. Adding an extra button and buttonhole or trouser hook and eye helps prevent horizontal stress lines from forming at the middle of the band and makes the closure more durable.

After you have sewn a buttonhole or trouser hook on the overlap with its corresponding button or eye on the underlap, add another buttonhole or hook on the end of the underlap, with its corresponding button or eye on the inside of the overlap, with the two sets of

fasteners about 1½ in. apart. When you sew that second fastener on the overlap, take care that your stitches do not show through to the right side of the band.

■ ADDING PLEATS TO PANTS

If you have a flat-front pants pattern that suits you but you would like to add pleats to it, this can be easily done with the following steps.

1. Extend the width of the front pattern piece only at the upper side seam from the full hip to the waist as you did for elastic-waist pants (see p. 93). Measure the increase at one side seam. Divide it by the number of desired pleats on one side of the pants front. For example, if you increased the waist by 4 in. and you want two pleats, each pleat needs to take up 2 in. of width at the waist.

2. Put the placement line of the innermost pleat on the pants creaseline. If it isn't marked on the pattern, fold the pants front piece in half lengthwise with the hem edges even and

Double closures work twice as well as single closures on plus-sized garments.

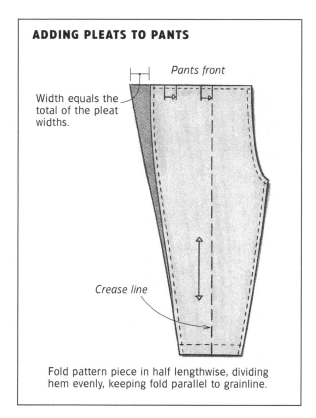

ADDING PLEATS TO PANTS

Pants front

Width equals the total of the pleat widths.

Crease line

Fold pattern piece in half lengthwise, dividing hem evenly, keeping fold parallel to grainline.

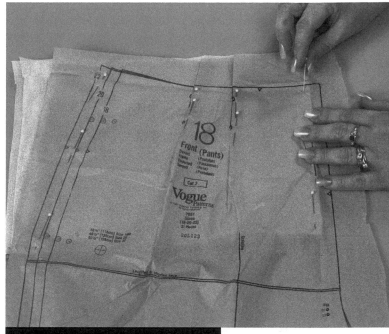

For back-zip pants, this power net stay is cut on the fold at the center front line. Its width matches the pants front after the pleats and center front seam are completed.

the fold parallel to the grainline; crease the pattern to mark.

3. To add a second or third pleat, divide the distance from the side seam to the first pleat to mark the other pleat placement lines.

4. Measure and mark the pleat take-up from the placement lines to the outer foldlines. For example, to take up 4 in. increased width into two pleats, the pleats need to take up 2 in. of width each, so each finished pleat will be 1 in. wide.

Remember that the distance between the folds of multiple pleats on the outside of the pants should look even, but the depth of the underlaps can vary because they do not show. You can adjust the width of the pleat underlaps to accommodate whatever increase in width

you want and still keep the outside folds of the pleats evenly spaced. For pants with three pleats on each side, for example, you could use two pleats that take up 2 in. each toward the middle of the front to accommodate your belly and another evenly spaced third pleat, ½ in. deep, toward the outseam of the pants for a total take-up of 5 in.

Staying pleats

To prevent pleats from forming diagonal stress lines over your tummy and to encourage them to drape in attractive vertical folds, you can stay them. Here's how to do it.

1. To cut a stay, pin the pleat foldlines to the placement lines on the pattern as for the finished garment. Use the adjusted pattern to cut

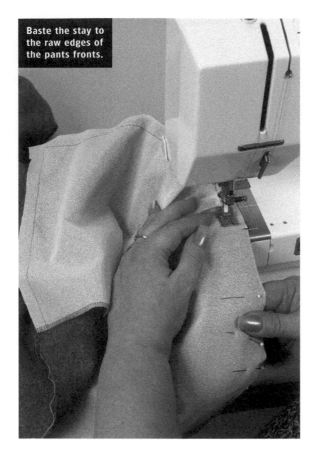

Baste the stay to the raw edges of the pants fronts.

tip *If you find that your stay cut on the fold tends to roll up when you are seated, use a French tack to anchor it to the crotch seam allowance.*

a stay of Lycra power net. Cut the stay long enough to reach your full hip level. Place it on the fold for back- or side-zippered openings (see the photo on p. 103). For front-zip pants, cut the stay the same shape as the center front seam.

2. After sewing the pleats in the pants, finish the lower edges of the stay, and baste it to the upper side seam, waist, and the upper center front seam allowances for pants with a center zip. Complete the garment as usual.

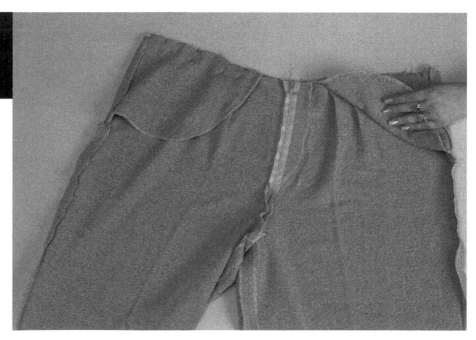

Side seam pocket bags also stay pleats. Note that the center front area is left unstayed to allow for belly spread when seated.

You can also use a stay on skirts with tucks or back-zip pants to prevent distortion from belly bulges. Cut the stay on the fold, and catch it into the side seams and waist seam.

If your pleated pants or skirt have side seam pockets, simply extend the width of the pocket bags so that when they're sewn into the waistband, they will back the pleats.

MAKING A FLAT-FELLED SEAM

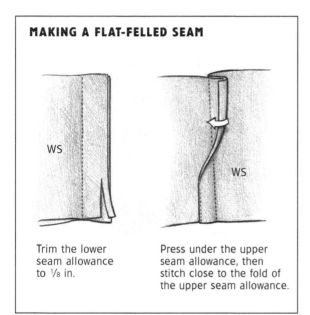

Trim the lower seam allowance to ⅛ in.

Press under the upper seam allowance, then stitch close to the fold of the upper seam allowance.

■ REINFORCED SEAMS

If you like a close fit on garments such as pants that are subject to wear and tear, you may wish to reinforce some of the seams. Typical stress areas in pants include the crotch seam, the upper inseam, and the side seam from waist to thighs.

A **flat-felled seam** looks sporty, wears tough, and is suitable for straight or gently curved seams. To make one, follow these steps.

1. Sew the seam with right sides together, and press it to one side.

2. On the wrong side, trim the lower seam allowance to ⅛ in., and then press the upper seam allowance under by ¼ in.

3. Stitch close to the pressed edge of the upper seam allowance, ⅜ in. from the original stitching line.

For **a mock flat-felled seam,** sew the seam, finish both seam allowances together by serging, zigzagging, or pinking firmly woven fabrics. Then press the seam to one side and topstitch ⅜ in. from the seamline.

MAKING A MOCK FLAT-FELLED SEAM

Topstitch on the right side of the garment.

⅜ in.

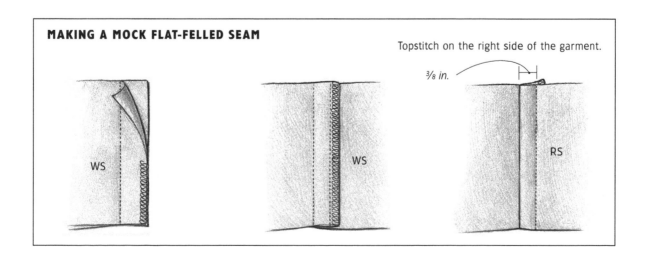

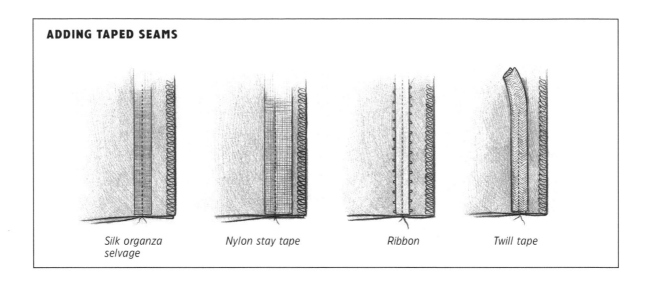

ADDING TAPED SEAMS

Silk organza selvage   *Nylon stay tape*   *Ribbon*   *Twill tape*

Taped seams

Taped seams are sturdy and fast to sew. You simply stitch a piece of stay tape onto a seam. The type of tape you choose should match the weight of your fabric. For example, ¼-in. twill tape is appropriate for heavy woolens or denim; a strip of selvage or narrow ribbon works for medium-weight fabrics; a length of sheer nylon tricot stay tape, a doubled strip of tulle, or a selvage of silk organza would be appropriate for sheers and other lightweight fabrics.

Use clear elastic to help prevent excess stretching and stress on seams for knits, especially at shoulder seams and crotch seams. Just serge or stretch and stitch right through the edge of the elastic as you sew the seam.

You can also use narrow strips of fusible interfacing along seamlines, matching the type of interfacing to the fabric. For example, you could use strips of fusible nylon tricot interfacing to stabilize stressed seams on knit garments.

■ SHOULDER PADS

Most plus-sized women look as if they have rounded shoulders, partly because the curve at the shoulder continues with the curve of our upper arms, making one great big curve, instead of dropping straight down as thinner arms do. That's why most of us look best with shoulder pads. Also, the wider the distance at the shoulder area, the narrower the width of our lower torsos will seem in comparison.

An **extended shoulder pad,** which juts over the arm about ½ in., is attractive because it allows the sleeve to drop straight from the shoulder seam to the fullest part of the upper arm. Because most plus-sized patterns are too long in the shoulder seam, it's unlikely you'll need to extend the shoulder seam or back and front in the chest area to accommodate a pad for an extended shoulder line. Instead, an extended shoulder pad, with its slightly longer than average length, will help support this area and enhance the silhouette of the garment.

UNDERLINING: THE ALMOST UNIVERSAL SOLUTION TO STICKY SEWING SITUATIONS

Underlining is an old-fashioned technique that can make an inexpensive garment look like a million bucks. It's frequently used in couture sewing but is seldom seen in ready-to-wear because it reduces profits for manufacturers by requiring extra fabric, time, and skill. For home sewers, however, underlining is very easy and doesn't take much time.

Underlining is simply an extra layer of fabric that is cut and stitched as one with the face fabric. There are many important advantages to underlining plus-sized garments.

• Underlinings help prevent seam slippage and strengthen all seams, particularly for fragile or loosely woven fabrics.

• A crisp underlining can change the hand of a fabric from droopy to drapey and can increase the apparent thickness of a fabric to make it seem more luxurious.

• Underlining helps reduce wrinkling and abrasion and protects the face fabric from perspiration and body oils.

• If a face fabric is scratchy, you can underline it with a soft fabric to make the garment more comfortable and eliminate the need for a lining. In this manner, an underlining serves as an alternative to a separate lining.

• If your fabric doesn't breathe well—for example, an evening dress made of polyester—a cotton batiste underlining next to the skin can increase your comfort.

• Underlinings modify the opacity of sheer garments. You can underline all or just part of a sheer garment, such as the bodice of an organza blouse with the sleeves left sheer. You can choose matching, skin-toned, or contrasting colors for underlining sheers; think of a black lace dress with a nude or hot pink underlining!

• Hems and facings can be "hung," in other words, hand-stitched only to the underlining so that hemstitches do not show on the outside. Try underlining your next satin skirt or gown for completely invisible hemstitches!

• You can even use bright prints and colors from your fabric stash for underlinings, if they don't show through to the outside, for a secret little pleasure every time you dress.

• Underlining hides construction details like darts, hem allowances, facings, and boning as well as underwear lines and body bulges.

Basic Method for Underlining

1. Cut an underlining for all the main pattern pieces, such as the bodice front, back, and sleeves or the skirt front and back. Always match the care requirements of face and underlining fabrics. If your face fabric is sheer, you may also want to underline "the little pieces"—collars, waistbands, facings, and so on—to maintain the design of the garment. If your face and underlining fabrics are the same width, you can cut both the garment pieces and the underlining at once. Just lay the two fabrics on top of each other, carefully aligning the foldlines and/or selvages. Then lay out your garment as usual, and cut both layers at once.

Sometimes underlining eliminates the need for additional interfacing; if needed, interfacing can be applied by fusing or stitching to the underlining rather than to the face fabric.

2. To join the underlining and face fabric layers together, press each piece, sandwich them together on a large, flat surface, and pin all around the edges. Don't be overly concerned if the edges don't line up precisely; just keep the pieces perfectly flat.

3. Baste the two layers together. For fragile fabrics, hand-baste just inside the seam allowance. For sturdier fabrics, use your longest machine stitch and loosen the needle tension to help avoid puckering and to make removing the stitches easier. On sturdy, washable fabrics and knits, you can also use a washable glue stick dotted around the edges of the pieces and dry the glue quickly with the heat of your iron.

4. Once joined, handle the two layers as if they were one garment piece and complete the garment as usual.

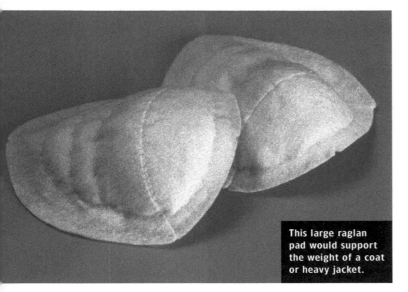

This large raglan pad would support the weight of a coat or heavy jacket.

Tailor's pads come in rights and lefts. The armscye edge is shaped to fit most jackets.

tip *For all kinds of shoulder pads, one size does not fit all! Select larger pads that fit the size of your shoulder. I like the resin-coated, preshaped poly pads that are fairly rigid. Soft, shapeless, fluffy pads do not work well. They perch on your shoulders like lumpy pillows.*

For an enhanced but natural-looking shoulder, choose **raglan shoulder pads** for dropped-shoulder, kimono, and raglan sleeves and for knit garments.

Use fluff-filled, canvas-covered **tailor's pads** for dry-clean-only jackets, coat dresses, and coats. Note that these pads are asymmetrical; the longer, narrower end is designed to clear your shoulder blades and goes toward the back of the garment.

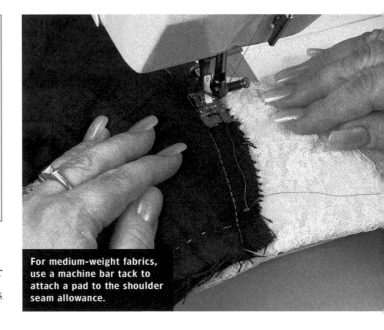

For medium-weight fabrics, use a machine bar tack to attach a pad to the shoulder seam allowance.

Attaching shoulder pads

To attach pads on washable garments made of medium-weight fabrics, start by trying on the garment. Position the pad into the sleeve even with the edge of the armscye seam allowance, and pin it in place at the shoulder seam. Remove the garment and bar-tack the center

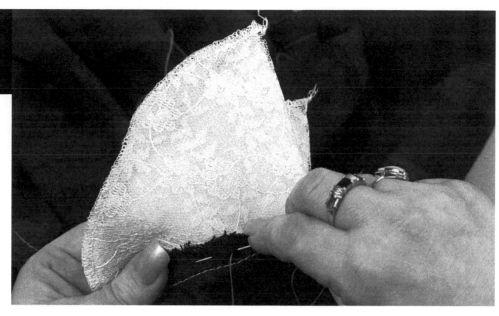

To avoid dimples with lightweight fabrics, sew pads to the shoulder seam allowance by hand.

COVERING SHOULDER PADS

To cover pads, use a square of your face fabric, lining, or underlining fabric. Place the shoulder edge of the pad on the diagonal, and fold the fabric over to enclose the armscye edge of the pad. Pin through all layers around the outer edge of the pad, stretching the cover on the bias to fit the curves of the pad. Serge (or zigzag and then pink) the outside edges, catching the pad edge slightly as you sew. Use skin-toned covers for translucent fabrics. Try a remnant of lace for an especially pretty pad cover.

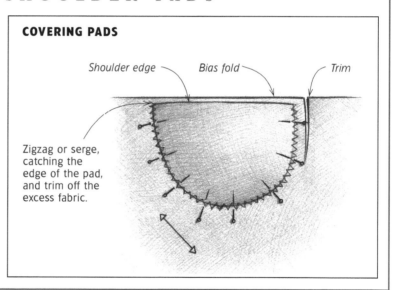

COVERING PADS

Shoulder edge — Bias fold — Trim

Zigzag or serge, catching the edge of the pad, and trim off the excess fabric.

of the neck edge and armscye seam edge of the the pad by machine to the shoulder seam allowance.

For thinner fabrics that might show a dimple on the outside where you would bar-tack through the compressible pad, just sew the pad by hand with a backstitch along the shoulder seam allowances. Let the lower corners of the pad swing free to avoid distortion on the garment from body movement.

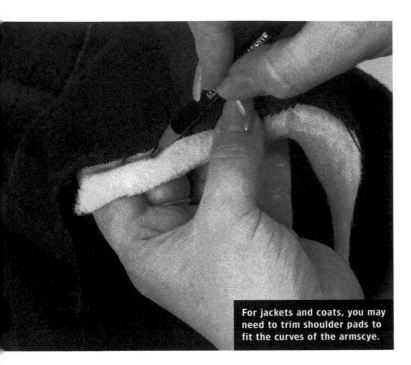

For jackets and coats, you may need to trim shoulder pads to fit the curves of the armscye.

Shaping shoulder pads

For tailored garments, if the pad is not shaped to fit the curves of the armscye, it can cause vertical sag lines on the front and back below the shoulder seams. There are two ways to correct this problem.

For resin-coated pads, you can stretch or snip and stretch the rounded edge of the pad until it lies smoothly without distortion. Since the back of the armscye is larger than the front, you may need to stretch the pad only in the back.

For these pads and for tailor's pads, you can also correct the shape of the armscye edge of the pad. Place the pad in the armscye before you attach the sleeve and hold it with one hand inside the garment. Scoot the pad into the armscye until the seam allowance covers the entire pad underneath, with some of the pad extending past the armscye seam allowance to accommodate its curves. With your other hand, mark the excess pad along the seam allowance, and trim it as marked. Attach the sleeve, and then reinsert the pad. Hand-sew the armscye seam allowances to the edge of the pad, and tack the center of the curved edge of the pad to the shoulder seam.

Adding pads to a pattern

If your pattern does not call for pads but you want to use them or if you want to increase the thickness of a pad, you need to draft sufficient height at the top of the sleeve cap and at the end of the shoulder seam to accommodate the width of the pad. For example, for a ½-in.-thick pad, raise the end of the front and back

ADJUSTING FOR SHOULDER PADS

Add for the thickness of a new pad or for the increase you want over the old one. For example, if your old pad is ¼ in. thick and your new pad is ¾ in. thick, increase the shoulder by ½ in.

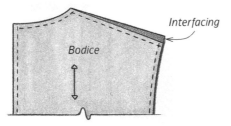

Interfacing

Bodice

If you want to add a ½-in.-thick pad to a pattern that does not call for pads, add ½ in. to the shoulder.

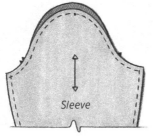

Sleeve

Add the thickness of a new pad or the increase over the old one to the sleeve cap.

tip *If you have one high shoulder, instead of adjusting the pattern asymmetrically to fit, which would emphasize the problem, simply use one relatively thicker and one thinner pad to achieve visual balance.*

shoulder seams by ½ in., and draw a ½-in.-higher sleeve cap. Any excess height can be fitted out later.

Keep in mind that the goal of shoulder pads is to help balance your proportions and to help support the weight and shape of tailored garments. Generally speaking, if you can "see" the pad from the outside, something is wrong. Experiment with the following methods until the pad fits smoothly over the shoulder and upper sleeve area without distortion.

• Try another size or shape of pad.

• Scoot or twist the pad around slightly.

• Stretch, clip, or trim it to fit the armscye curves.

• Try a different attachment method.

■ CLOSURE PLACEMENT

If your mobility is restricted or even if your arms are too short to reach around easily to your center back to fasten buttons or zip up zippers, it's easy to relocate openings for blouses, pants, and dresses to the center front for easier access. (See the drawings on p. 112 for options when eliminating a back closure.)

1. Adjust the back pattern piece to eliminate the closure. For straight center back seams, such as on a loose blouse or dress, you can just trim the back pattern piece at the center back line, and place it on the fabric fold to eliminate the center back seam. Discard whatever back facing or seam allowance you have trimmed off. For shaped center back seams, such as on a fitted dress, keep the seam allowance at center back.

2. To convert to front-buttoned closure with a cut-on facing, look at the center front line on the front pattern piece. You must add additional width equal to the width of the buttons you plan to use; then mark the new foldline.

To convert to front-buttoned closure with a sewn-on facing, add width to the original center front line equal to the width of the buttons plus a seam allowance; draw the new cutting line.

To convert to a zip front, just add a seam allowance to the center front foldline, and insert the zipper into the new seam as usual.

3. Draft the new front cut-on or sewn-on facing. For both kinds of facings, tape tissue under the center front area of the garment from the hem to the longest part of the upper edge of the pattern to the shoulder seam. Fold the tissue along the center front foldline for cut-on facings and at the cutting line for sewn-on facings. Then draw new cutting lines for the desired width of the new front facing up to the shoulder seam cutting line. Follow the pattern instructions to sew the facings on the fronts the same way as for the backs.

4. Last, trace a new back facing using the bodice back piece. Place tracing paper on the

ELIMINATING A BACK CLOSURE

TRIMMING OFF THE BACK FACING

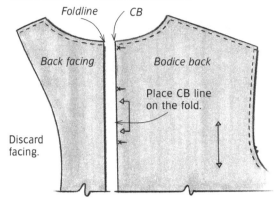

Foldline   CB

Back facing   *Bodice back*

Place CB line on the fold.

Discard facing.

For straight CB seams, trim off the back facing and eliminate the CB seam.

ADDING A NEW CUTTING LINE

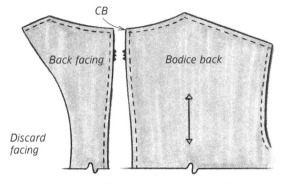

CB

Back facing   *Bodice back*

Discard facing

For shaped CB seams, discard the back facing and retain the seam allowance at the CB.

DRAFTING A SEWN-ON FRONT FACING

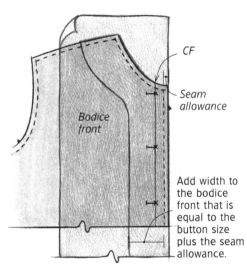

CF

Seam allowance

Bodice front

Add width to the bodice front that is equal to the button size plus the seam allowance.

DRAFTING A CUT-ON FRONT FACING

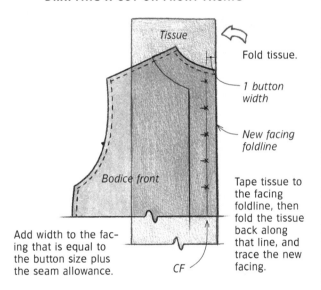

Tissue

Fold tissue.

1 button width

New facing foldline

Bodice front

Tape tissue to the facing foldline, then fold the tissue back along that line, and trace the new facing.

Add width to the facing that is equal to the button size plus the seam allowance.

CF

DRAFTING A NEW BACK NECK FACING

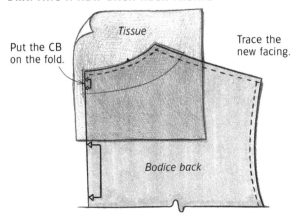

Tissue

Put the CB on the fold.

Trace the new facing.

Bodice back

foldline at center back, and draw a back facing, maintaining the same width at the shoulder as for the front facing.

You may want to change zipper locations from center back to the left side seam for skirts or pants or to center front for pants in the same manner as steps 1 and 2 on p. 111, only there's no facing to fiddle with. On skirts with straight center back seams, cut the back on the fold to save sewing time.

■ BUTTON PLACEMENT

If you sometimes suffer from dreaded "gapiosis" when you wear dresses or blouses with a center front buttoned closure, you probably don't have enough width across the bust area. However, you may also need to correct the buttonhole and button placement so that one button is level with the apex mark on your pattern and the fullest part of your bust on the garment. Place the topmost button wherever it is marked on the pattern. Then place a button at the fullest part of the bust, in line with the apex mark on the pattern.

For larger, more widely spaced buttons, measure the distance between the first and second buttons, and space the rest accordingly. For smaller, more closely spaced buttons, place another button halfway between the first one and the one at the bust, and use the distance between the buttons to place the rest. When possible, place a button or other fastener at the waist to prevent gaping below the bust. You can mark the corrected button placement on the pattern or on the nearly completed garment.

Place one button level with the bust apexes. Notice that for this loose-fitting tunic, the vertical draping below the bust apexes functions as waist darts, worn here as ease.

■ THE MAGIC OF GUSSETS

The word "gusset" may sound unfamiliar and scary, but it just refers to triangular, diamond-shaped, or rectangular-shaped pieces of fabric inserted into seamlines to add length and width for fit, comfort, and movement (see the top left photo on p. 115). Dance costumes, for example, are nearly always sewn with underarm gussets for added mobility. Adding a gusset to a set-in or kimono sleeve allows a closer

A ZIPPY ZIPPER FOR ZINGY CENTER FRONTS

A mock-fly, center front zipper is fast and sporty on jeans skirts and pants and creates extra vertical lines to break up width across the hips. Follow these steps.

1. Before cutting the pants fronts, draft a fly extension on the front pattern piece at center front about 2 in. wide, curving to about $\frac{1}{2}$ in. below the lower zip stop location; for a 9-in. zipper, this would be about 10 in. down from the waistline.

2. On the right pants front, fuse interfacing to the extension just past the center front line.

3. On the left pants front, trim off the extension at the original cutting line.

4. Partially sew the center front crotch seam from the point where you wish to place the end of the lower zipper stop to within 1 in. or 2 in. of the other end of the front crotch seam. You will complete the crotch seam later. Then finish the fly extension and seam allowances.

5. Next, press the left center front seam allowance to the inside by a scarce $\frac{1}{2}$ in., forming a $\frac{1}{8}$-in. pleat at the end of the opening, which allows the fly to cover the zipper completely by $\frac{1}{8}$ in. on the finished garment.

6. Use a zipper foot to topstitch the zipper in place close to the fold of the left center front seam allowance. Fold the fly extension to the inside along the center front line of the right pants front, and press.

7. Lay the fronts right side up on your ironing board. Overlap the fly to the underlap by $\frac{1}{8}$ in., covering the topstitching on the left hand side of the zipper, and pin or baste in place along the fly fold. Close the zipper.

8. Turn the fronts to the wrong side, pin the free zipper tape to the extension, and stitch it to the extension only.

9. Finally, fold the extension back in place, baste it around the finished edge, and topstitch about $1\frac{1}{4}$ in. from the fold, curving to meet the center front crotch seam just below the zipper stop. Finish with a horizontal bar tack for durability.

10. Complete the pants by sewing the fronts to the backs at the inseams as usual, then sew the entire crotch seam, overstitching the previous stitching at the front crotch by 1 in. or 2 in.

ADDING A MOCK FLY

ADDING THE FLY EXTENSION

Left pants front — WS

Right pants front — WS

Trim off of left front after both pieces are cut.

SEWING IN THE ZIPPER

Sew left zipper tape.

Scarce $\frac{1}{2}$ in.

$\frac{1}{8}$-in. pleat

WS

Right fly extension

Align the left zipper teeth to the fold, and stitch.

1. Close zipper.
2. On the right side, lap the fly over the left zipper by $\frac{1}{8}$ in. Pin along the fold.
3. Pin the right zipper in place on the fly extension only.
4. Open out the extension, and stitch the zipper tape.

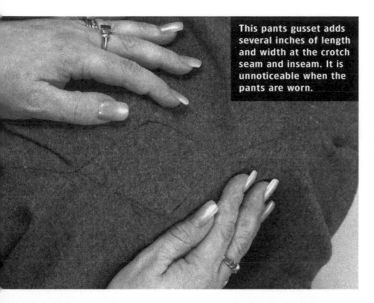

This pants gusset adds several inches of length and width at the crotch seam and inseam. It is unnoticeable when the pants are worn.

Reinforce the ends of the four seams.

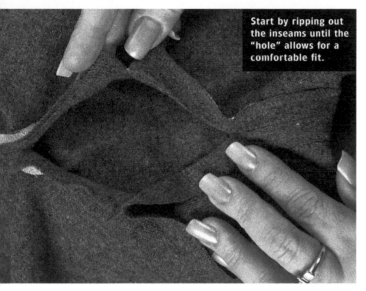

Start by ripping out the inseams until the "hole" allows for a comfortable fit.

fit at the underarm and increases movement. You can also add them to the crotch seams of pants; in fact, you may have to add them if your pattern pieces are wider than your fabric. If you have garments that are tight or binding in the crotch or under the arm or that you have "outgrown," you can add gussets to increase length and width and make them wearable again.

Here's the basic method for adding a gusset.

1. To add an underarm gusset to a top, first rip out a couple of inches of the side seam and sleeve seam where they intersect the armscye seam at the underarm area. For pants, rip out a couple of inches of each inseam where the inseams intersect the crotch seam (see the bottom left photo). You will have to rip out a few stitches on the crotch seam or underarm lower armscye seam to do so.

2. Try the garment on to check for comfort. Let out the seams a bit more, if needed. Note that the hole you have created is roughly diamond shaped.

3. Next, fuse a small piece of interfacing to the wrong side of each of the eight seam allowances where the stitching stops to reinforce these areas. To secure the broken stitches

Pin the gusset to fit the opened seams.

Sew with the gusset down, holding the seam allowances out of the way, so you can see exactly where to stop at the gusset corners. Backstitch and break the thread before sewing the next side of the diamond.

GUSSETS IN DESIGN

Try using gussets made of two-way stretch fabrics for activewear. For example, picture a contrasting, triangular-shaped Lycra gusset running down the side seam of a quilted ski bib.

If you don't have enough fabric to match your garment, try contrasting colors and work the new color elsewhere into the design. You could repeat the shape and color of a contrasting underarm gusset with diamond-shaped appliqués, pockets, triangular-bound buttonholes, or other design features.

For rectangular side-seam gussets to increase garment width, instead of matching fabric, you could insert lace trim or ribbon the width of the necessary increase.

USING GUSSETS IN DESIGN

Binding/contrast trim piping

Underarm gusset

Triangular-bound buttonholes

Pocket with triangular point trim

Repeat the shape of the contrasting gusset elsewhere in the design.

at the end of the four seams, sew over the original stitching for a couple of inches, and backstitch at the end of the opening (see the right photo on p. 115).

4. Then cut an elongated diamond-shaped gusset, with the narrowest width of the diamond on the crossgrain and larger than the opening in the split seams.

5. Pin the two corners in line with the short width of the gusset to the crotch seam breaks for pants and to the armscye seam break for sleeves. Pin the longer points to the inseams or to the sleeve seam and side seam break for tops (see the left photo on the facing page).

6. Adjust the gusset and the seam allowances until the gusset fits the opening.

7. With the gusset facing down, stitch the layers together, backstitching at the beginning of each of the four seams, and backstitching then breaking the thread at the end of each of the seams (see the right photo on the facing page). Fold the seam allowances out of the way and do not catch them in the gusset seams.

8. Trim and finish the seams.

■ SLITS AND VENTS

It's easy to add slits to the side seams of tunics or slits or vents to the center back or side back seams of jackets to allow for comfort while seated. That's why equestriennes' jackets are always vented—they're made for sitting!

For a slit, simply sew the side seam to just below the waist, backstitching to reinforce the end of the seam. Finish the entire length of the

seam, press it open, and then press the open edge along the seamline. Alternately, turn under the seam allowance by ¼ in. Topstitch the opening, pivoting at the upper edge of the slit, bar-tacking horizontally as you reach the seam, and pivoting again to complete the top-

Bar-tack as you reach the top of the slit to reinforce the seam and continue topstitching the slit.

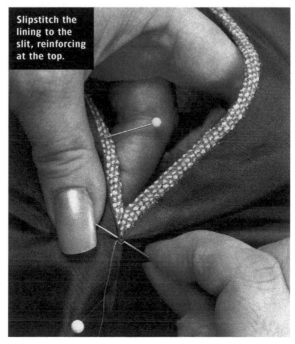

Slipstitch the lining to the slit, reinforcing at the top.

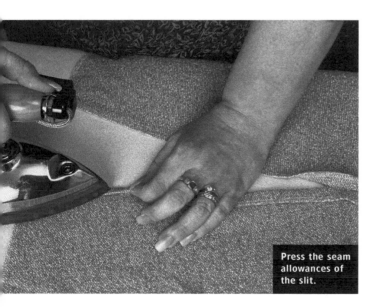

Press the seam allowances of the slit.

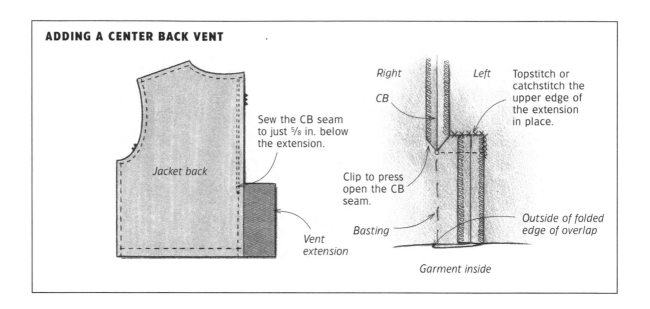

ADDING A CENTER BACK VENT

Jacket back

Sew the CB seam to just ⅝ in. below the extension.

Vent extension

Right   Left   Topstitch or catchstitch the upper edge of the extension in place.

CB

Clip to press open the CB seam.

Basting   Outside of folded edge of overlap

Garment inside

Secure the overlap with topstitching at the top of the vent.

stitching (see the top right photo on p. 117). For lined garments, don't finish or press under the seam allowances an additional ¼ in. around the opening. If applicable, sew the lining seam a bit shorter than the corresponding seam on the face fabric, and press under seam allowances. Slipstitch the lining an even ¼ in. from the folded edge, match the two seamlines at the top of the stitch, and take a few hand stitches across the lining seam at the top of the slit (see the bottom right photo on p. 117).

For a center back vent, first draft a rectangular extension, about 2⅝ in. wide and the desired length, usually the length from the waist to the hem for jackets. Tape the extension to the pattern lower center back seam, and cut out the back pieces. Sew the center back seam up to a point ⅝ in. into the extension. Then diagonally clip the *right* seam allowance only into the extension close to the end of the seam so you can press the center back seam open. Press the extension toward the *left* back. Finish and press under the long edges of the left and right extensions.

Lay the vent over a flat surface, and baste the overlap in place. Topstitch across the upper ends through all layers, pulling the thread ends to the inside to knot them. Or, catchstitch the extensions in place invisibly on the inside. Hem the long edges of the extensions when you hem the garment, mitering the corners.

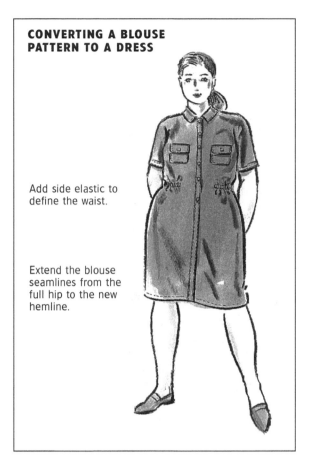

CONVERTING A BLOUSE PATTERN TO A DRESS

Add side elastic to define the waist.

Extend the blouse seamlines from the full hip to the new hemline.

CONVERTING A JACKET PATTERN TO A COAT DRESS

Extend the pattern from the full hip to the desired hem length; add buttons as desired.

■ ADAPTING BASIC PATTERNS TO MAKE OTHER GARMENTS

Once you have spent your valuable time adjusting patterns, make them work even harder for you. For example, you can **convert a basic, dart-fitted bodice or princess-lined blouse to a dress** just by lengthening the side seams and the center front and center back lines from the full hip to your desired hem length. Or, you can slash and spread a bodice on a shirtwaist dress with an elastic waist to **produce a blouson bodice.**

For a jacket pattern that fits you well, just lengthen at the seamlines to **sew a coat dress** at whatever hem length you desire. To **convert to an outerwear coat,** also widen the garment somewhat and lengthen the armscye and sleeve cap to loosen up the fit.

Once you have a basic straight skirt adjusted for your figure, **convert the skirt to an A-line** by flaring the side seams from the full hip to the hem. Draw a curved line from the extended side seam to meet and match the curve of the lower skirt edge (see the top drawing on p. 120). To **make a four-gore flared skirt,** flare both the front and back side seams from the full hip to the hem. Add a seam allowance to the foldline at center front, then flare the center front and center back cutting lines an amount equal to the flare at the side

CONVERTING A STRAIGHT SKIRT TO AN A-LINE SKIRT

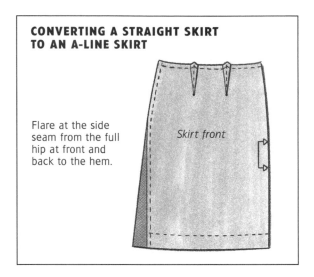

Flare at the side seam from the full hip at front and back to the hem.

Skirt front

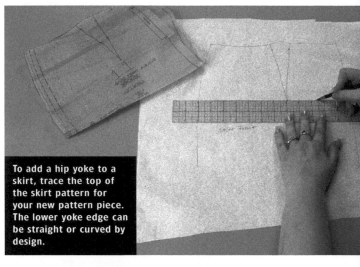

To add a hip yoke to a skirt, trace the top of the skirt pattern for your new pattern piece. The lower yoke edge can be straight or curved by design.

CONVERTING A STRAIGHT SKIRT TO A 4-GORE SKIRT

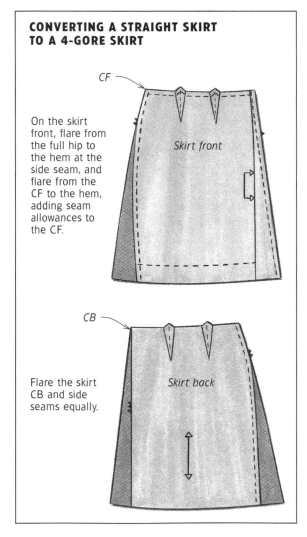

CF

On the skirt front, flare from the full hip to the hem at the side seam, and flare from the CF to the hem, adding seam allowances to the CF.

Skirt front

CB

Flare the skirt CB and side seams equally.

Skirt back

Close the dart on the new yoke piece. Note that the yoke is now a dart equivalent.

seams from the waist to the hem; curve the lower edges.

Try **adding a hip yoke to gathered, pleated, or circle skirts** to be worn under long tops to reduce bulk. Start by tracing the upper part of your basic skirt pattern. On the tracing paper, draw in the desired shape of the lower edge of the yoke at whatever distance from the waist that will work for the top you want to wear. Add a seam allowance to the lower edge. Cut out the waist darts on the tis-

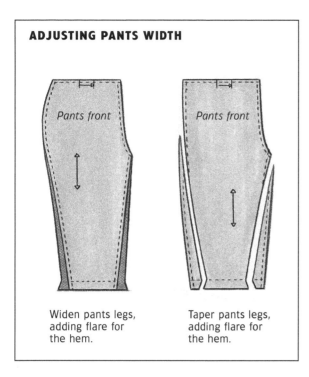

ADJUSTING PANTS WIDTH

Pants front

Widen pants legs, adding flare for the hem.

Pants front

Taper pants legs, adding flare for the hem.

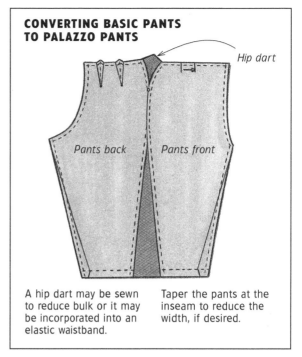

CONVERTING BASIC PANTS TO PALAZZO PANTS

Hip dart

Pants back   *Pants front*

A hip dart may be sewn to reduce bulk or it may be incorporated into an elastic waistband.

Taper the pants at the inseam to reduce the width, if desired.

sue the same way you cut out bust darts when you rotate them (see p. 83). Slash from the vertex of the darts to but not through the lower yoke seamline, then close the darts, and tape them in place. Notice that the lower yoke now curves and has become a dart equivalent.

You can manipulate a pants pattern that you like to **make other pants styles.** For a tapered leg, just draw a diagonal line on the front and back pattern pieces from the full hip to the hem on the side seams and from the upper inseam downward to narrow the pant equally on each side of the leg. Remember to flare out the seams slightly from the hemline to the lower cutting line to allow for the angles of the leg taper when you turn up the hems. Use the same technique to widen the legs of a tapered pant.

To **make palazzo pants with no side seams,** which are comfortable and graceful in a lightweight, drapey fabric, lay your front and back pattern pieces on your cutting surface. Keeping the grainlines perfectly parallel, overlap the seamlines at the full hip, and tape or pin in place. Notice the hip dart that forms! You can sew this as a curved dart to reduce bulk, or you can leave it in for an elastic waistband. For extra fullness, you can also spread the two pieces apart, keeping the grainlines even. Connect the upper waistlines and lower cutting lines, as shown in the right drawing above. You can taper these pants slightly, say for sweatpants, at the inseams to reduce fullness if desired.

Now that you've adjusted your pattern for your body size, figure variations, and the design modifications you wish to make, you can cut the garment out and get ready for your fitting.

a basted fitting: the only way to get it right!

■ ■ 8 ■

Please, do not even think about skipping the basted fitting! With a big mirror, good lighting, and patience, you can easily fit yourself. Having a helper such as a sewing friend can be wonderful if he or she understands the fitting process or is trainable. If your vision or mobility is impaired or if you would just like some help, consider hiring a sewing professional to help you with fittings (see Appendix B on p. 142). Use a dress form for fittings if and only if it accurately reproduces your size and shape.

Don't worry that you'll have to adjust for all of the fitting criteria described in this chapter. If you have adjusted for your body size and figure variations, you may need to make only one or two fast adjustments at this point.

ZEN DRESSMAKING

Weather forecasters, despite their sophisticated computer programs and scientific equipment, know that there is no substitute for sticking their head outside and looking at the sky. They also accept that they cannot get every forecast right because weather is a tremendously complex system with just too many variables.

Sewing is the same way. Every garment you will ever sew is quintessentially unique, just like today's weather. Sewing is a joyous and magical immersion into the dynamics of design, materials, construction techniques, and fit. In a way, it's a bit arrogant to think that we ought to be able to get a garment cut and sewn right the first time we try, even with careful calculations and planning. Instead of assuming that we can understand and control everything, it may be wiser and easier at this point to simply step back, look at our garments, and allow the materials we use to tell us what to do. This is a point of view I affectionately call "Zen Dressmaking." In this light, a fitting is a time to listen to what our garments are telling us.

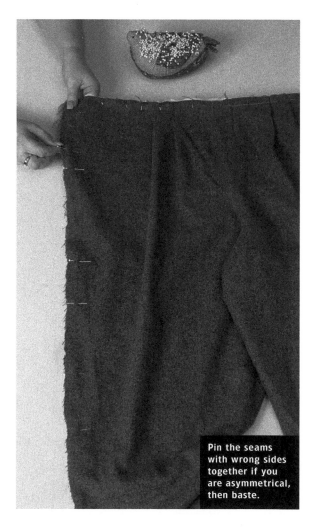

Pin the seams with wrong sides together if you are asymmetrical, then baste.

tip *Pin-fitting a pattern on a dress form or onto your body doesn't work very well for large people. It's not very accurate because the pins torque and seamlines gap. Tissue tears easily, and it doesn't drape like your fabric. Pins can jab you. It is easier, faster, and far less painful to baste!*

■ BASTING THE GARMENT FOR A FITTING

Here is how to baste a garment in preparation for a fitting.

1. To start, cut the garment out and transfer all construction marks as usual to the garment wrong side with chalk or a fabric marker, or to both sides with thread tacks or tracing. Staystitch all neck, waist and other stretchy edges to prevent distortion during construction and fitting.

2. If your figure is symmetrical, pin the main garment sections with right sides together. If your figure is asymmetrical, pin the garment sections with wrong sides together (see the photo on the facing page).

3. Set your machine for its longest stitch, loosen the needle tension, and hold the fabric slightly taut in front of and behind the needle to avoid puckered stitches. For stretch fabrics, baste with a long, medium-width zigzag, keeping the left hand swing of the needle on the seamline.

4. Baste all darts, tucks, and pleats, then baste all vertical seams and intersecting horizontal seams, such as shoulder seams, yokes, or waist seams. Leave zips and other closures open so you can try the garment on. Break the thread wherever the seams and darts intersect, so you can easily adjust them while fitting.

> **tip** *Baste by hand if your fabric is fragile like lace or chiffon. Make a knot in the end of the thread, sew long running stitches along the seamline, and take a large backstitch at the end of the seam. To remove the basting, just pull out the backstitch, grab the knot, and pull out the basting thread. Many sewers prefer hand basting for a fitting because the stitches are so fast and easy to remove.*

> **tip** *Cut muslin to test-fit a garment only if any of the following situations exist.*
> • *Your fabric is extremely expensive.*
> • *You have custom-drafted the pattern by hand or computer.*
> • *You have enlarged the pattern radically, more than four sizes.*
> • *Your garment has elaborate geometric seaming.*
> • *You have made extensive, extreme adjustments for figure variations.*
> • *Your body is extremely asymmetrical.*

On the left, the unfitted jacket sags across the upper chest, the dart is too high for the correct apex position, and the torso area from the armscye down forms vertical sag lines. On the right, pinning the neck edge of the shoulder seams deeper, lowering the upper end of the dart, and taking in the side seams allows the fabric to flow over the body smoothly.

5. Try the garment on over the same kind of underwear you'll wear with the completed garment, and wear shoes with the same heel height. Heel height affects posture, which affects fit. If you are symmetrical, the seams and wrong side of the garment should be on the outside; if you are asymmetrical, the right side of the fabric and seams should be on the outside.

6. Accurately pin the closures shut by placing pins on the seamline, parallel to the cut edge and end to end, so the opening will not gap. If the closure is in the back, try pinning the opening partially shut before you slip the garment on. Feel the seam allowances and look in the mirror to judge where to pin the remainder of the opening accurately. In the same manner, overlap buttoned closures and place pins through all layers to match up the button and buttonhole marks correctly. Insert shoulder pads, if applicable, and pin them in place. Now look in the mirror.

7. Check every location listed below that applies to your garment *in the order given*. Note that a fitting proceeds from the top of a garment downward—sometimes correcting a problem with the shoulder seam, for example, also eliminates other fitting problems elsewhere on the garment.

■ FITTING FROM THE WAIST UP

Generally, unwanted horizontal wrinkles or stress lines on a garment indicate that there is not enough width across the body area covered. These lines tell us to let out the vertical seams in that area. Unwanted vertical wrinkles, or sag lines, indicate that there is too much width across an area. Take in at the vertical seams to correct this. Diagonal lines form when there is something wrong with both length and width; they nearly always point toward the problem.

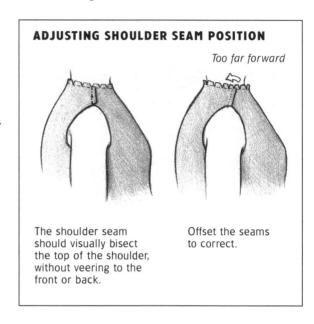

ADJUSTING SHOULDER SEAM POSITION

Too far forward

The shoulder seam should visually bisect the top of the shoulder, without veering to the front or back.

Offset the seams to correct.

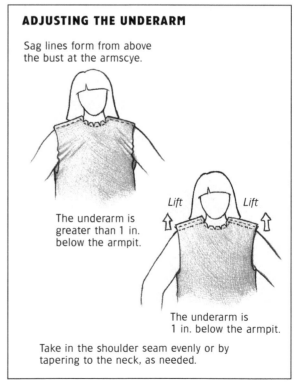

ADJUSTING THE UNDERARM

Sag lines form from above the bust at the armscye.

The underarm is greater than 1 in. below the armpit.

Lift   *Lift*

The underarm is 1 in. below the armpit.

Take in the shoulder seam evenly or by tapering to the neck, as needed.

Shoulders

The shoulder seam should ride the top center of the shoulder and bisect the shoulder area when viewed from the side or from above, without veering to the front or back. Clip the basting, offset the seams, and repin, if needed. Note that you will check the length of the shoulder seam later, when you check the arm-scye position.

Now look at the underarm. For a set-in sleeve, the lower part of the seamline should fall about 1 in. below the armpit for garments with sleeves and about ½ in. for sleeveless garments. If it is too low, lift up the garment at the shoulder seams and pin a deeper seam. If the underarm is too high, it will feel binding or uncomfortable. You can let out the shoulder seam evenly or scoop the underarm a bit lower. Kimono and raglan sleeves have lower armholes by design, unless they are gusseted.

Next, look at the upper front of the chest and across the upper back for stress lines from

> **tip** *Surprisingly, the higher the underarm for a set-in sleeve, the easier it is for the arm to move without restriction. In ready-to-wear, arm movement is often hampered by large, long armscyes. Ready-to-wear manufacturers frequently rotate shoulder darts to the back armscye and bust darts to the front armscye and do not close them up as darts to save labor costs.*

ADJUSTING THE UPPER CHEST

STRESS LINES FORM FROM SHOULDER TIP TO TIP

Shoulder tip

Let out the shoulder seam at the shoulder tip.

SAG LINES FORM AT THE ARMSCYE ABOVE THE BUST

Shoulder tip

Take in the shoulder seam at the tip, tapering to the neckline.

ADJUSTING A JEWEL NECKLINE

Let out.

Take in.

The neckline is too tight—stress lines form vertically.

The neckline is too big—sag lines form and the neckline gaps.

Let out or take in at the shoulder seam; alternately, scoop the front neck lower.

shoulder tip to tip. Let out the shoulder seam at the shoulder tip until the stress lines disappear, and taper the seam to the neckline.

If unwanted diagonal lines form at the armscye above the bust, take up the shoulder seam at the shoulder tip, tapering to the neckline.

Neckline

For jewel necklines, vertically clip the seam allowance to the staystitching to release the curve. Is the neckline uncomfortable or binding? Let the shoulder seam out at the neck edge or scoop the neckline lower and wider to adjust. To do so, remove the garment, fold it in half lengthwise at the center front neckline, and cut the neck curve slightly deeper and wider. Staystitch the new neckline, and try it on. If a neckline gaps, take it in at the neck edge of the shoulder seam, and/or stay it. Remember to mark corresponding changes on collars and facings.

Next, take a look at the back of the neckline.

If there is extra fabric gapping at the back neckline over a rounded upper back, for example, pin out the excess as two neck darts so that the back neckline snugs the neck and upper back smoothly. Remember to adjust the back facing or collar if you adjust the back neckline.

Width across the chest

For a natural shoulder line, check that the armscye seamline follows a fairly straight-looking line, close to perpendicular to the floor, from the top of the shoulder bone to the armpit. For an extended shoulder, it should slant slightly outward, and for a narrow shoulder design, slightly inward. Palpate the top of the arm to find the spot where the shoulder blade meets the shoulder joint, just as if you were cutting up a chicken.

If needed, use a marking pen, chalk, or thread tracing to mark a new armscye seamline from

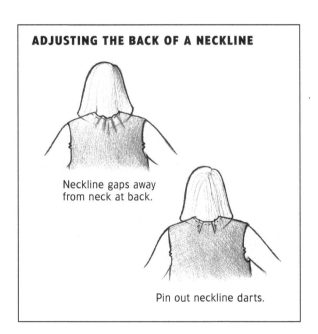

ADJUSTING THE BACK OF A NECKLINE

Neckline gaps away from neck at back.

Pin out neckline darts.

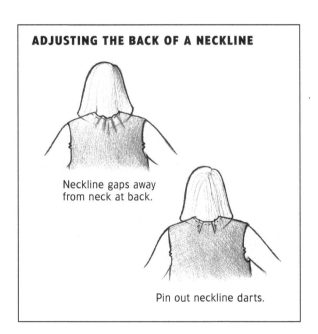

STAYING A SCOOP OR V-NECKLINE

Scoop or V-necklines may need staying to prevent gapping. To stay a neckline, run a gathering stitch by hand or machine at the seam-line of the opening, and pull it tight enough to distribute the ease evenly along the neckline until it no longer gaps. Then baste a stay tape on the wrong side over the basting, taking care to ease the neckline to the tape and avoid puckers. Carefully press the neckline to shrink it to the tape.

ESTABLISHING SHOULDER SEAMS

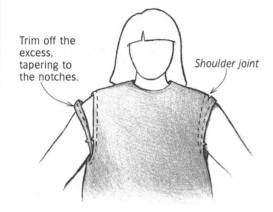

Narrow

Natural

Extended

ADJUSTING ARMSCYE SEAM POSITION

Trim off the excess, tapering to the notches.

Shoulder joint

Feel for the shoulder joint to establish the natural shoulder seam location.

tip *Don't confuse design lines in the form of draping, gathers, pleats, tucks, shirring, and so on with unwanted wrinkles that indicate fitting problems. Also, always allow for both design and fitting ease. Do not overfit!*

ADJUSTING BUST DARTS

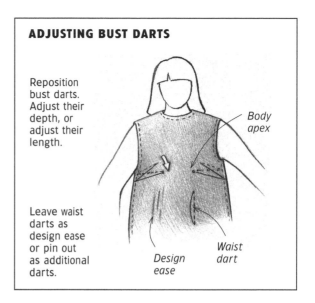

Reposition bust darts. Adjust their depth, or adjust their length.

Body apex

Leave waist darts as design ease or pin out as additional darts.

Design ease

Waist dart

the corrected end of the shoulder seam, blending to the armscye front and back notches.

Bust darts

The bust darts should point to the fullest part of the bust and should end about 1 in. from the apex. Clip the basting, and reposition, lengthen, or shorten the darts, as needed. The bodice should conform to the shape of the bust smoothly without forming wrinkles. If needed for a large bust, clip the basting and fold the darts deeper or pin out additional darts, as needed; pin them in place. Note that waist darts are often worn as design ease for a loose fit or as gathers or tucks on waisted dresses.

Princess seams across the bust

Generally, most princess seams should curve over the apex of the bust. If they do not, clip the basting, and offset the seams over the bust area to adjust. The curve of the princess seams should also skim the curve of the bust below

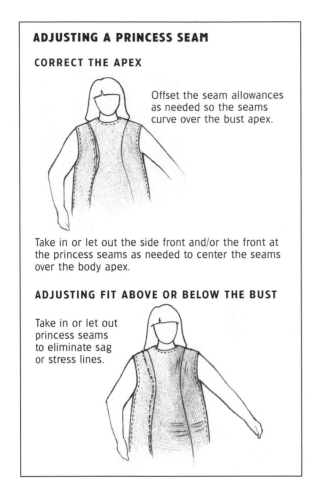

ADJUSTING A PRINCESS SEAM

CORRECT THE APEX

Offset the seam allowances as needed so the seams curve over the bust apex.

Take in or let out the side front and/or the front at the princess seams as needed to center the seams over the body apex.

ADJUSTING FIT ABOVE OR BELOW THE BUST

Take in or let out princess seams to eliminate sag or stress lines.

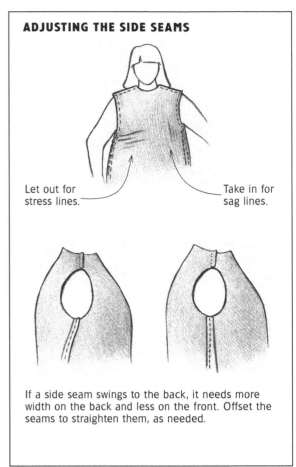

ADJUSTING THE SIDE SEAMS

Let out for stress lines.

Take in for sag lines.

If a side seam swings to the back, it needs more width on the back and less on the front. Offset the seams to straighten them, as needed.

and above the apex, without compression or sagging. Some princess seams fall toward the center front or toward the side seam by design. Take in or let out at the princess seams and upper side seams as needed to accommodate the curve and circumference of the bust area. Stiff and thick fabrics are often more difficult to ease into the tightly curved, closely fitted princess seams on larger cup sizes. There is a limit to the amount of ease and the degree of curve that is possible to sew without puckering. If you haven't drafted an underarm dart on the pattern to accommodate a large bust, you can try straightening out the curve of the princess seams slightly and letting out the bust area at the side seams so the fabric skims but does not closely fit the figure.

Now look at the princess seam from the apex to the armscye or shoulder seam where it ends. Pin out any excess fabric above and then below the bust as needed. Note that princess seams that end at shoulder seams should generally bisect the shoulder seamline. If needed, offset the seams to center them between the neckline and the tip of the shoulder.

Remaining vertical seams to the waist

The side seams should hang perpendicular to the floor. If they do not, offset the seams, and repin so that they hang straight. Look for horizontal pull lines that indicate tightness or vertical sag lines that indicate excessive looseness. Take in or let out at the side seams as needed. For princess-seamed garments, distribute any width adjustments evenly among the seams.

If you carry your weight more in front than in back, the side seam is more attractive if it visually bisects the body than if it intersects the low center point on the armscye, as viewed from the side. Adjust the seam position if needed.

Center back seam

If a fitted garment has a center back seam, it should skim the curves of the upper and lower back smoothly without horizontal stress lines that indicate tightness or sag lines that either indicate too much width or too much length, such as for a swayback. Adjust as needed.

Sleeve cap

At this point, rebaste the shoulder seam and side seam down to the waist along whatever adjustments you have already made, using the pins as guides. Then baste the right sleeve seam, and baste the sleeve into the right armscye. It's fastest to do this by hand because you can ease and baste at the same time with a running stitch. If you are asymmetrical, baste in both sleeves. Insert both shoulder pads, if any, and pin them in place. Now look at the sleeve. If the cap forms horizontal stress lines from notch to notch, there is not enough width in that area. Let out the armscye seam in the chest area front and back, tapering from the notch to the end of the shoulder seam to increase width.

If the cap forms a collapsed indentation below the shoulder pad, you may need to let out the seam allowance on the sleeve all around the sleeve cap from notch to notch to increase both length and width over the upper arm (see the left drawings on p. 132).

If the sleeve cap sags vertically or puckers or if it was difficult to ease into the armscye, there is too much length and width. Remove the basting, and rebaste the sleeve with a slightly wider seam allowance on the sleeve cap only,

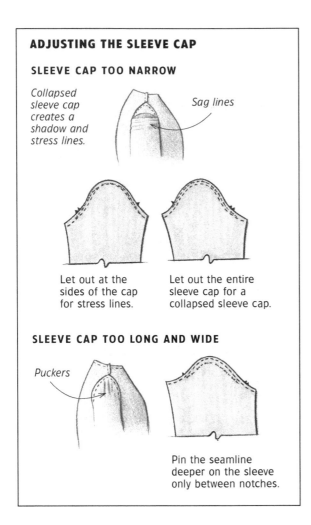

ADJUSTING THE SLEEVE CAP

SLEEVE CAP TOO NARROW

Collapsed sleeve cap creates a shadow and stress lines.

Sag lines

Let out at the sides of the cap for stress lines.

Let out the entire sleeve cap for a collapsed sleeve cap.

SLEEVE CAP TOO LONG AND WIDE

Puckers

Pin the seamline deeper on the sleeve only between notches.

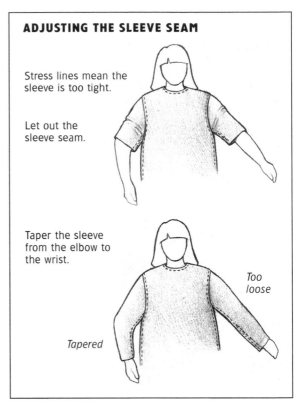

ADJUSTING THE SLEEVE SEAM

Stress lines mean the sleeve is too tight.

Let out the sleeve seam.

Taper the sleeve from the elbow to the wrist.

Too loose

Tapered

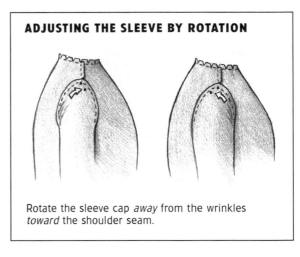

ADJUSTING THE SLEEVE BY ROTATION

Rotate the sleeve cap *away* from the wrinkles *toward* the shoulder seam.

---

from notch to notch, until the cap fits the armscye smoothly.

Sleeve seam

If needed, take in or let out in the upper arm area so the sleeve fits smoothly without tightness or bagginess. Generally, you should be able to "pinch an inch" at the sleeve seam for 2 in. of wearing ease at the upper arm. If the lower end of a long, plain sleeve is too wide and flaps about the wrist, taper it from the elbow to the hem, remembering to flare out the end of the

sleeve seam in the hem allowance slightly to accommodate the taper of the sleeve.

For two-piece sleeves, check that the sleeve curves comfortably toward the front to wherever your arm naturally falls at rest. If wrinkles form on the front or back of the sleeve cap near

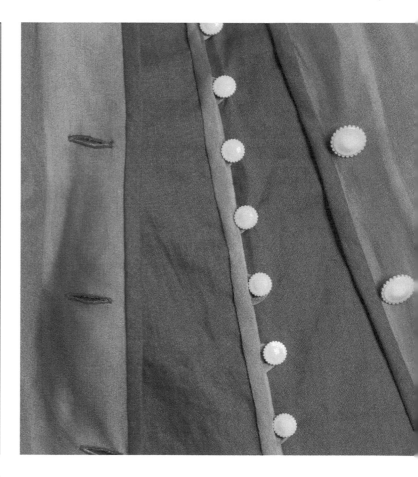

Let out the seams at the back armscyes and the upper CB, tapering at the end of the shoulder seam and notches.

tip
Dress forms do not usually have arms! If you are using one, remember to baste in a sleeve and try the garment on. If you want to add an "arm" to your dress form to help with fitting, use a long-sleeve pattern with an elbow dart. Cut it out in muslin, fit it tightly to your arm, and sew the darts and sleeve seam end. Stuff the arm with polyfil, and sew an oval-shaped piece of muslin to cover the opening in the arm from underarm to shoulder. Attach the stuffed arm to the dress form with pins or duct tape.

the notches, remove the sleeve from the armscye and rotate the sleeve cap slightly in the armscye, from the wrinkles toward the shoulder seam. Lastly, gently bend your arms forward and feel for straining across the back. If this is uncomfortable, let out the back at the armscyes and center back seam, if any, to correct.

Button placement

Check the front for correct button positions, as described on p. 113. Mark the center front where it is level with your apexes. Adjust the button positions as needed to prevent gapping. Generally, larger buttons are spaced wider apart than smaller buttons.

If you adjusted your pattern at the upper side seam and armscye to increase width across the bust and you increased the same amount at the upper sleeve seam, you should have plenty of width at the upper arm.

If you have large, football-shaped upper arms, you will end up with an armscye that is as large as the circumference of your upper arm, so you can pull the sleeve on. However, this can result in an armscye that is too big, particularly in front. A bubble of excess fabric will form at the armscye seam between the chest and the bust. It looks as if you should dart the excess out on the bodice and the sleeve, but that would probably result in an armscye that would be too small for you to pull the garment on comfortably.

To correct this problem, take the sleeve out of the armscye, and put the bodice back on. Pinch out an armscye dart on the front and on the back as needed to fit the armscye smoothly to the body. This will make the armscye smaller, but now the sleeve will be too large for you to ease it into the armscye. You can't reduce the sleeve width or it might not fit your upper arm. Instead, repin the sleeve into the armscye about 1/2 in. *inside* the armscye stitching line on the bodice at the end of the shoulder seam.

Gradually increase the seam allowance in width at the notches, and then flatten out the seamline level with the lowest point of the old armscye. The new seamline on the bodice will look like the silhouette of your pressing ham propped up on its wide end.

This results in a larger armscye circumference to fit your large upper arm without lowering the armhole. Baste the sleeve back into the armscye. Widen or narrow the width of the lower armscye seam allowance at the level of the notches (the bottom of the ham shape) as needed to make the seamline fit your sleeve.

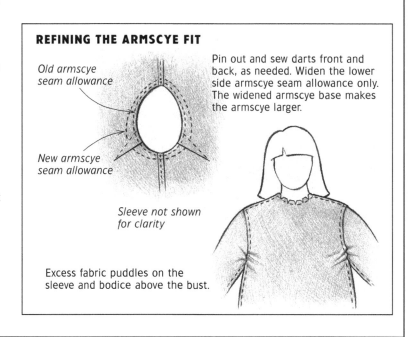

REFINING THE ARMSCYE FIT

Old armscye seam allowance

New armscye seam allowance

Sleeve not shown for clarity

Excess fabric puddles on the sleeve and bodice above the bust.

Pin out and sew darts front and back, as needed. Widen the lower side armscye seam allowance only. The widened armscye base makes the armscye larger.

■ FITTING FROM THE WAIST DOWN

Baste the vertical seams, darts, or dart equivalents, like tucks or pleats. For pants and skirts, baste on a temporary waistband of 7/8-in. grosgrain, 1-in. elastic, or a combination to correspond with your waistband style. Break the stitching at the seams and darts or equivalents so they are easy to manipulate while fitting. Try the garment on, and pin the closure shut. Lap the temporary waistband, and pin in place.

Waistband

The waistband should be perfectly level all around the body. Look in the mirror sideways

tip *Use a long, medium-width zigzag to baste elastic. The zigzag stitch will allow the temporary band to stretch around the waist during the fitting, as elastic in casings will on the finished garment. Long zigzag basting stitches are easy to remove after the fitting.*

to check. To adjust, clip the basting at the temporary band, and reposition it on the pants or skirt so it is level; pin it in place.

If you have one high hip and one low one, lift the waist of the garment on the low side and reposition the band over the excess fabric at

ADJUSTING THE WAISTBAND POSITION

Reposition the waistband so it is level from front to back.

Lift the garment at the low hip, and reposition the waistband to keep it level.

High hip   Low hip

the waist so the band is level; pin the band to the adjusted garment waist on the low side.

Side seams from the waist down

Take in or let out at the side seams to fit the curve of the side of the hips and to eliminate stress lines or sag lines (see the drawings at left on p. 136). For fitted styles, you should be able to "pinch an inch" at each hip for a minimum of 4 in. of wiggle room.

The side seams should fall perpendicular to the floor. If they don't, check that the waist is level. If it is, remove the basting, offset the seams so they fall straight, and pin them in place.

Remember that skirts with design ease, such as pleated or full, gathered styles, may have yards of ease: Do not fit it out! Pants with pleats and gathers at the waist also have extra design ease that you must retain.

Darts

Below the waist, darts and their equivalents, such as tucks, pleats, or gathers, should point to

tip *If side seam or slant pockets pull open on finished garments, the skirt or pants are too tight at the upper hip and waist. Let out the side seams at the hips and waist until the pockets lie flat. If you have a very rounded and protruding belly, slant pockets will call attention to this roundness. Inseam pockets may be more flattering for your figure.*

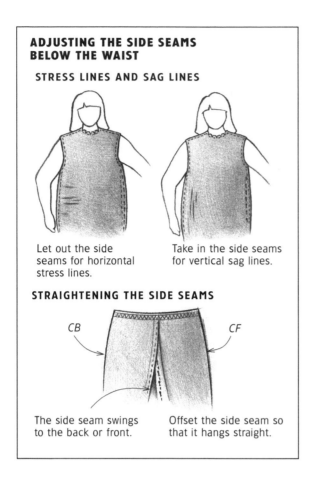

ADJUSTING THE SIDE SEAMS BELOW THE WAIST

STRESS LINES AND SAG LINES

Let out the side seams for horizontal stress lines.

Take in the side seams for vertical sag lines.

STRAIGHTENING THE SIDE SEAMS

CB

CF

The side seam swings to the back or front.

Offset the side seam so that it hangs straight.

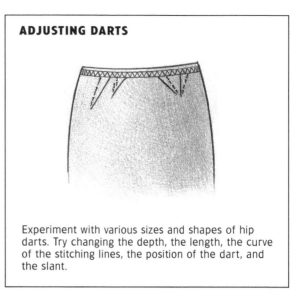

ADJUSTING DARTS

Experiment with various sizes and shapes of hip darts. Try changing the depth, the length, the curve of the stitching lines, the position of the dart, and the slant.

the fullest part of the curves they accommodate, either the belly or the buttocks. If you adjusted your pattern for additional width at the waist and hips, you may need to shift the darts or their equivalents right or left. Ideally, their position should visually bisect the area between the center front and side seams.

You may need to take in or let out the depth, or take-up, of waist darts. You may need to shorten or lengthen them to accommodate your unique body shape. Or, you may need to repin their straight stitching lines as curved lines—usually concave at the small of the back or convex over the belly. The finished dart lines can be slanted slightly from the waist toward

the side seams, or they can point straight down. If you have large hips and a relatively small waist, you may want to redistribute one large dart as two or more smaller waist darts.

Remember that darts or their equivalents are just extra folds of fabric that form as we wrap two-dimensional fabric around our three-dimensional, round bodies. Just use your fingers to smooth out wrinkles, and pin out the excess as darts as needed to eliminate sag lines.

Crotch seam

That four-point juncture of the crotch seam and inseam should hang at least 1 in. below the body for flat-front pants and up to 4 in. for pleated or gathered styles.

If the crotch is too short, it will pull down the waistband at center front and back, and the crotch seam will bind uncomfortably, forming "smile lines" at the crotch. This means that you didn't adjust your pattern for crotch length, or you didn't adjust it for a protruding tummy or

Even if you are potato- or apple-shaped and your waist is as large as your hips, do not eliminate darts or their equivalents. You still need them, however shallow, to fit the roundness of your belly and the curve of your lower back. Darts and their equivalents also create flattering vertical lines and help create the illusion of a waist.

fanny. To correct, try adding a gusset, as explained on p. 113.

If the crotch is ridiculously droopy, just lift the pants at the waist, and reposition the temporary waistband. Recheck the darts and side seams at the hips. You will probably need to adjust their depth and length, and you will probably need to adjust the curve of the side seams.

Then take a look at the pants back. If you have a flat fanny, you may have extra fabric sagging below the fullest part of your backside. To correct, clip the basting at the upper inseam and take in the back inseam only until the sagging disappears. You may also need to shorten the crotch length at the upper back by clipping the waistband stitches, lifting up the pants center back until the sag lines disappear, and repositioning the band.

ADJUSTING THE CROTCH LENGTH

Lift the pants at the waist.

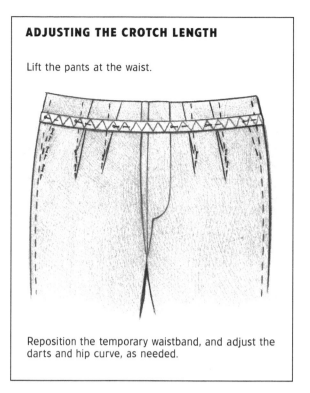

Reposition the temporary waistband, and adjust the darts and hip curve, as needed.

ADJUSTING THE PANTS BACK

If you have a flat fanny, take in the pants at the back inseam.

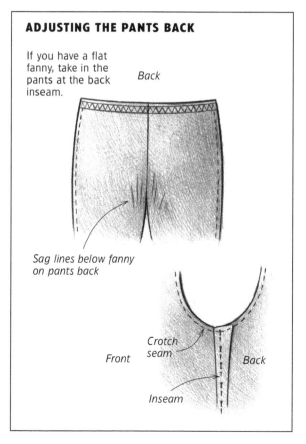

Back

Sag lines below fanny on pants back

Front *Crotch seam* *Back*

Inseam

Leg taper for aesthetics

If pants legs are too full for your taste, you can taper them equally at the side seam and inseam, as described in Chapter 7. Generally, pants in soft fabrics, such as challis or crepe, look best with wider legs and a looser fit, which also places less stress on the seams of these relatively fragile fabrics. Stiff or crisp fabrics, on the other hand, such as denim, duck, or crisp linen, look best made up as relatively narrow-legged pants. A slightly closer fit also helps reduce the appearance of bulk for pants made in these thicker, heavier fabrics.

Placement of design features for aesthetics

Check the location and scale of buttons, pockets, and other ornamentation. You may wish to change the location and size of patch pockets, for example, from the hips to the chest on a

tip *Use transparent tape to place buttons, trim, or pockets in place temporarily so you can see how they will look on the finished garment. Consider the scale of these design features. Would buttons, trim, or pockets look better if they were larger? Cut paper samples in larger sizes, and tape them to the garment to evaluate the overall scale. Also, experiment with the placement of pockets and trim. Would patch pockets at the bust look better at the hip if you are apple shaped?*

tip *Fitting a garment is like hanging wallpaper. Even walls that look straight, flat, and plumb never really are, so you make sure that the vertical seams are perpendicular to the floor and you use your hands and a brush to sweep away wrinkles and bubbles toward the seams. Fitting is exactly the same! The desired result is a garment that skims the figure smoothly and comfortably, without wrinkles, puckers, or sags that distract from the garment design.*

jacket or dress, if you are pear shaped, and you may want to enlarge them to balance your hips visually. In general, you may find that design features and trims that are a bit larger than recommended on the pattern will harmonize with the scale of your body.

Double-check the fit

At this point, if you have made extensive changes, carefully remove the garment. Using the pins as guidelines, rebaste all the adjusted areas. Put the garment back on and check the fit again. Try slowly sitting down, bending over, stooping, and stretching to check for comfort. Let out any area that feels tight or uncomfortable.

■ AFTER THE FITTING

Once your garment is pinned and basted the way you want it, take the time to mark all the changes you made during the fitting on your pattern. If you make up the garment again in a similar weight of fabric, you shouldn't need to refit! On the other hand, if you change the hand of the fabric, you must refit. A basic pants pattern made from a heavy woolen will not fit the same as the same pants in crepe de chine.

Then sew the garment permanently, following the pattern instructions. If your figure is symmetrical and the seam allowances are on the wrong side of the garment where they belong, sew closely alongside but not on top of the basting for easier removal. Remove the basting as little as possible as you sew intersecting seams in order to follow correct construction protocol. Trim the seam allowances to an even width and finish them as usual. Then remove the basting.

If your body is asymmetrical and the seams are on the right side of the basted garment, use chalk, a marking pen, or thread tracing to mark the new stitching lines on the wrong side only. Remove the basting, turn the pieces to right sides together, and construct the garment as usual.

The result of all your labor will be a garment that fits your unique body comfortably and attractively, that enhances your appearance and self-esteem, that expresses your sense of style, and that will bring you joy for many years. Remember that you deserve fine-quality clothing. Sewing your own is the best way to get it right!

appendix a: fashion figures for plus-sized designs

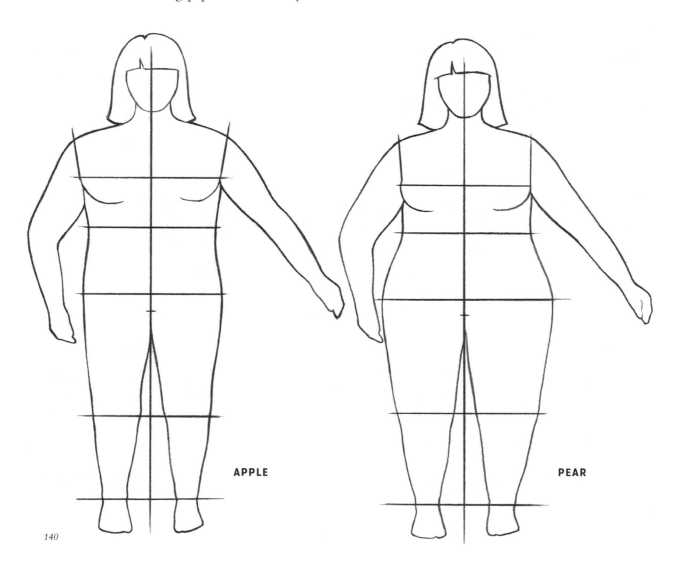

Fashion illustrators often trace idealized fashion figures as they draw. Select the realistic figure that looks most like you. Cover the page with a sheet of tracing paper and sketch your design over the figure. With a copy machine, you can also enlarge your fashion figure, make copies, and sketch directly on your copies.

APPLE

PEAR

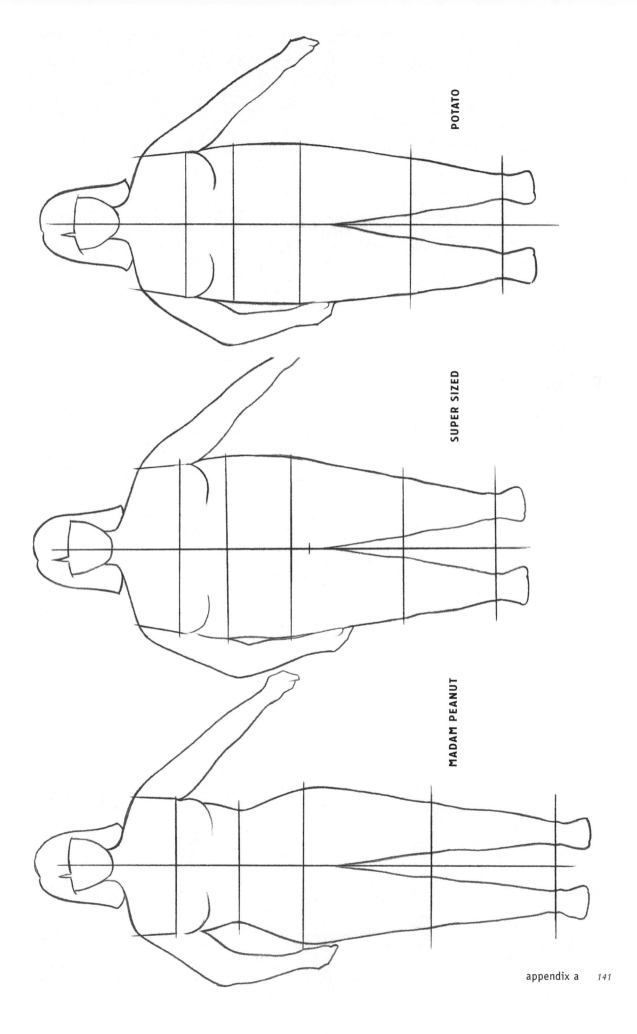

POTATO

SUPER SIZED

MADAM PEANUT

appendix b: how to find, select, and work with a custom clothier

Have you ever wished you could enjoy the pleasure of owning clothing made just for your size and shape without doing all the work yourself? You can!

Have you promised to make your daughter's wedding dress but are concerned that if the gown doesn't meet her high expectations, you will end up strangling each other? Even though you may be completely comfortable sewing sportswear, a formal evening gown may require techniques that you have never even tried before.

Are you in dire need of high-quality tailored clothing for the office but you're working 14-hour days and don't have time to sew? A sewing professional would suit you perfectly. It takes far less time to make a couple of brief visits to your dressmaker for fittings than it does to spend hours every weekend shopping.

Do you love to sew and love clothes that fit well, but you have trouble adjusting the pattern or doing a fitting? A sewing professional could custom-draft a pattern or could adjust a commercial pattern to fit your dimensions and figure variations.

Most of us busy women are accustomed to giving all our energy and attention to others in our family and workplace. Have you ever wished that somebody would do something wonderful just for you? A custom clothier could be that somebody.

■ A NOTE ON JOB TITLES

A *sewing professional* is the broadest term for anyone who makes her living in the sewing world, by sewing, teaching, writing, retailing sewing supplies, and so on. She may work full- or part-time in a retail shop, in a studio, or out of her home. She may be any or all of the following:

- A *custom clothier* makes garments one at a time to meet a customer's specific needs and preferences.
- A *custom dressmaker* generally specializes in women's custom apparel and may make day dresses, careerwear and suits, eveningwear, sportswear, or lingerie.
- A *tailor* makes custom menswear-style jackets and the skirts or trousers that go with them for men or women.

- An *alteration specialist* adjusts the fit of completed garments or restyles them.
- *Designers* think up combinations of proportion, line, texture, and color. They may work in the ready-to-wear industry, and they may or may not sew or do custom designing for individuals.
- *Patternmakers, sample makers,* and *fitters* are professionals who usually work in the ready-to-wear world but may offer services to individuals.
- *Home decorative sewing specialists* sew custom draperies and other soft furnishings.
- *Wardrobe consultants* or *fashion advisors* may clean out a client's closet, recommending flattering colors and styles to meet her needs.
- A *wearable artist* produces uniquely embellished garments; for her, a piece of clothing is a canvas.
- A *seamstress* is someone who sews seams; this term is sometimes used as a synonym for dressmaker. It often refers to a machine operator in a garment factory, who may not have the skills to make an entire garment from scratch. Please do not call your dressmaker a seamstress! Seamstress is also an old euphemism for prostitute. In pioneer Seattle, for example, 80 percent of the city's revenues at the turn of the century came from taxes on "seamstresses," who placed sewing machines (instead of red lights) in their windows to advertise their profession. No doubt respectable dressmakers and tailors moved their machines away from the windows and had to sew in the dark.

■ HOW TO FIND A DRESSMAKER

One of the best ways to find a dressmaker is by word of mouth. If you know anyone who has used professional sewing services and you admire her clothes, ask her for the name of her dressmaker; you may have to twist her arm (gently, of course) since some women want to keep their dressmaker all to themselves.

Fabric stores often display business cards of local dressmakers and may be able to direct you to someone most likely to meet your needs.

Many dressmakers have enough work from word of mouth that they do not need to advertise, but check the Yellow Pages under "Dressmakers," "Designers," "Tailors," "Wedding Services," or "Bridal Shops," depending on your needs. You may also find ads in national and local fashion or bridal magazines or in newspapers.

You can contact the Professional Association of Custom Clothiers for a free referral to a sewing professional in your area (see Resources on p. 149).

Once you have a few names, gather up a paper and pencil so you can take notes, give these dressmakers a call, and ask them a few questions.

Find out her specialties

Some custom clothiers are willing and sufficiently skilled to sew almost any project that comes their way, from fixing a popped button to restyling a mother's wedding gown to custom-drafting a tuxedo pattern or designing an elaborate evening dress. However, most custom clothiers specialize. A particular dressmaker, for example, may only sew wedding gowns. A tailor may also do alterations. A designer may custom-sew a design for you, but a dressmaker may not also be a designer. Note that the skills of designing, pattern drafting, dressmaking, and tailoring are complementary, yet separate skills.

Some dressmakers may not be comfortable working with plus-sized women. That may not be because of bigotry but may be because they simply haven't had much experience with plus sizes. When you first call, ask what type of sewing she specializes in, and ask if she is adept at working with your size.

If the dressmaker's specialties meet your needs, make an appointment to see her.

Most dressmakers start with a consultation, which is a time for the two of you to get to know one another. The fee for this may be a separate charge, it may be refunded upon completion of your first garment, or it may be included in her pricing.

Many dressmakers measure you during the consultation, or they may make a separate appointment. Her measuring technique should be thorough and accurate, similar to the method described in this book.

Determine her qualifications

Ask the dressmaker about her training and experience. Although many sewing professionals have attended a design school, many with very high skill levels have been mentored by talented family members, sewing teachers, or employers, or they may be self-taught. Experience does make a difference. The longer we do this, generally speaking, the better we get.

Ask about her professional affiliations. As a rule, reliable dressmakers want to be accountable to their peers as well as to their clients. Professional organizations establish standards and provide opportunities for education, resources, and networking that improve the quality of services the dressmaker offers.

Be sure that she uses written estimates and contracts. The contract should itemize all materials that you will provide and whatever materials she will supply. It should itemize costs for materials and labor. It should list the date started, the date needed, and the date completed. It should exhaustively describe whatever work is to be done and even how it is to be done. For example, will the seams be run through a 3/4-thread serger, stitched, finished, and pressed open or flat felled? Remember that a contract protects both you and the dressmaker from misunderstandings.

Ask to see any sales tax or occupational licenses that may be required in your area. Never deal with anyone who is working "on the side," "under the table," or "off the books"—that person is not a professional!

Understand the process of dressmaking

Dressmakers usually do two or three fittings; she should explain the process to you. It should be similar to the method in the last chapter. The number of fittings vary with the complexity of the garment and whether or not she custom-drafts the pattern.

```
WORK AGREEMENT

BUSINESS NAME_____
DRESSMAKER NAME _____
BUSINESS ADDRESS_____
BUSINESS PHONE_____

CUSTOMER NAME _____
DATE _____
ADDRESS_____
CITY _____ STATE ____ ZIP _____
PHONE (H) (    )_____
        (W) (    )_____

PROJECT _____
PATTERN #_____

CONSTRUCTION/SKETCHES

DATE IN _____
DATE NEEDED _____
DATE COMPLETED _____

YARDAGE RECEIVED _____/_____
FIBER CONTENT _____
DRY CLEAN           WASH _____
FINDINGS RECEIVED_____
FINDINGS PURCHASED  $ _____
                    $ _____
                    $ _____
ESTIMATED LABOR   HRS _____
ACTUAL LABOR      HRS _____
                      _____
FINAL COSTS: _____
                      _____
LABOR AT $      /HR.  $ _____
                       _____
                       _____
                       _____
                       _____

          SUBTOTAL $ _____
         SALES TAX $ _____
                    _____
            TOTAL $ _____

DEPOSIT/CONSULTATION
FEE REFUND          $ _____

BALANCE DUE UPON
COMPLETION OF GARMENT $ _____

CUSTOMER SIGNATURE _____

DRESSMAKER SIGNATURE _____
```

Ask about timing. Most dressmakers require six to eight weeks for most garments, longer for multiple garments, and about six months for very elaborate projects such as wedding gowns or dresses for the wedding party. This may vary with the dressmaker and the time of year. Try to think a season ahead: Have your fall things made in the summer! If you need a garment in six weeks or less, ask if there is a rush charge.

She should explain your responsibilities: Do you select the pattern, fabric, and findings from samples in her studio, or do you find these on your own? Does she offer shopping assistance for an additional fee, or does she give you printed information to help you find fabric? Does she prefer to select the inner structuring elements such as interfacing, shoulder pads, and so on, based on her experience?

Examine her portfolio

During the consultation, the dressmaker should offer to show you her portfolio or garment samples. Bear in mind that her portfolio may consist of professionally photographed garments displayed on a dress form or a professional model, or it may consist of unretouched snapshots of garments worn by her ordinary-looking clients, who tend to pick up their completed garments wearing no makeup, with woozy hair and crew socks. Try to look at the garment, instead of the pretty face. Does it fit? Is it attractive? Are there plus-sized clients? Does she have letters of recommendation and thank-you notes from happy customers?

Learn about pricing

You should expect custom clothing to cost more than a comparable off-the-rack garment. If you shop at discount stores, that price may seem high. If you shop at luxury department stores or designer boutiques, the price may seem like a bargain. Custom goods of all kinds cost more than mass-produced goods. Bear in mind that you are not just buying a dress; you are hiring a highly skilled professional to produce a unique garment that meets your special needs.

Generally, custom-clothing prices are commensurate to the skill, experience, and reputation of the dressmaker and to the labor required to complete the garment that you need. A "jacket," for example, could be a simple unlined cardigan jacket in a solid color, sewn with budget, industrial techniques that might require 2 to 4 hours of labor, or it could be a hand-tailored, lined, and underlined menswear-style jacket with four welt pockets, ten bound buttonholes, three vents, and hand-applied trim in a plaid fabric, which might take 40 hours of labor or more. The dressmaker must understand your needs in great detail before she can fairly quote you a price. She may charge by the garment or by the hour.

Note that only about 20 percent of the retail price of an off-the-rack garment covers labor and materials; all the rest goes toward profits for the designer, manufacturer, and retailer and covers licenses, import fees, salesclerk's wages, retailer's rent, advertising, and other overhead factors. With custom-made clothing, on the other hand, all you pay for is the labor and materials, which is what you actually get to wear!

In addition, custom clothiers usually use much finer sewing techniques, at the level of luxury ready-to-wear, than those seen in "moderate" or "bridge" apparel. If you select fine fabrics, the result is a garment with much greater value.

Do not choose a dressmaker solely by price! If you have budget restrictions (don't we all), tell her your price range and ask for her suggestions. She may be able to suggest fabrics, designs, and sewing techniques that will produce a satisfying garment without breaking your budget.

During the consultation, ask her about her payment policy. Most dressmakers request a deposit with the contract and payments at each fitting.

Your responsibilities

Select fine quality fabrics for your custom clothing. It makes no sense to use cheap fabrics with expensive labor. Take care to communicate your needs and desires clearly; she cannot read your mind! Also, please be on time for fittings. Your dressmaker is as busy as you are! If you need to reschedule appointments, do so far in advance. Always bring the foundation garments and shoes you will wear with your custom garment to fittings.

Lastly, when your first garment is completed, you are happy with it, and you have enjoyed the dressmaking process, take a minute to write a note to your dressmaker. Your payment may help buy the groceries, but your compliments will feed her soul.

further reading

■ SIZE ACCEPTANCE

Books

Erdman, Cheri K. *Nothing to Lose: A Guide to Sane Living in a Larger Body.* San Francisco: Harper, 1995. Written by a plus-sized psychcologist.

Fraser, Laura. *Losing It: America's Obsession with Weight and the Industry That Feeds on It.* New York: Dutton, 1997. A thoroughly documented exposé of the $70 billion a year diet industry.

Gaesser, Glenn. *Big Fat Lies: The Truth about Your Health and Your Weight.* New York: Ballantine, 1996. Much published in scientific and medical journals, Gaesser asserts from his point of view as a physiologist and scientific researcher that no scientific studies to date have proven that fatness in and of itself is unhealthy. He recommends that if you are concerned about your health, you should reduce the fat in your diet, eat more fiber, fruits, and veggies, and get more exercise. Good advice!

Johnson, Carol A. *Self-Esteem Comes in All Sizes: How to be Happy and Healthy at Your Natural Weight.* New York: Doubleday, 1995. Well documented.

Magazines

Big Beautiful Woman (BBW). Bimonthly. A nice-looking and easy-reading mix of fashion, beauty, size acceptance, and interviews with plus-sized celebrities. Some super-sized models. For subscriptions, call (800) 707-5592, or write BBW, P.O. Box 458, Mt. Morris, IL 61054. Web site: www.bbwonline.com; E-mail: bbw@lfp.com

Belle (Black Elegance Presents the Magazine for Full-Figured Women). Quarterly. Fashion, beauty, and size acceptance; some super-sized models; great style and attitude in the fashion spreads. For subscriptions, call (800) 877-5549, or write Belle, 475 Park Avenue S., New York, NY 10016. E-mail: QQHZ34A@prodigy.com

Mode. Bimonthly. A slick new fashion and beauty magazine for the smaller end of the plus-sized range (12,14,16, etc.). Young, fun, and stylish; sophisticated fashion photography. For subscriptions, call (212) 328-0180, fax (212) 328-0188, or write Mode, 22 East 49th Street, 5th floor, New York, NY 10017. E-mail: modemag@aol.com

Radiance Magazine: The Magazine for Large Women. Quarterly. Mostly size acceptance, some fashion and beauty, interviews with accomplished plus-sized women and celebrities. For subscriptions, call (510) 482-0680, or write Radiance Magazine, P.O. Box 30246, Oakland, CA 94604.
Web site: www.radiancemagazine.com
E-mail: RadMag2@aol.com

Organization

The National Association to Advance Fat Acceptance (NAAFA). Quarterly newsletter, national and regional conferences, local chapters. Their literature states that their issues are advocacy, education, and support. For more information, write NAAFA, P.O. Box 188620, Sacramento, CA 95818; (800) 442-1214; E-mail: naafa@naafa.org

■ DESIGN

Mason, Carla, and Helen Villa Connor. *The Triumph of Individual Style: A Guide to Dressing Your Body, Your Beauty, Your Self.* Menlo Park, CA: Timeless Editions, 1994. Great pictures of art portraying voluptuous women; wardrobing from an artist's perspective. To order, call (415) 321-5997.

Zangrillo, Frances Leto. *Fashion Design for the Plus Size.* New York: Fairchild Publications, 1990. Fashion design, pattern drafting, and grading from an industrial point of view.

■ SEWING AND PATTERNMAKING

Cabrera, Roberto, and Patricia Meyers. *Classic Tailoring Techniques: A Construction Guide for Men's Wear.* New York: Fairchild, 1984. Fine hand-tailoring techniques and fitting; applicable to women's suits.

Crawford, Connie. *The Art of Fashion Draping,* 2nd ed. New York: Fairchild, 1996. Teaches patternmaking by draping on a dress form.

Kopf, Ernestine, and others. *How to Draft Basic Patterns,* 4th ed. New York: Fairchild, 1991. Basic flat-pattern drafting.

Kopf, Ernestine, and others. *Designing Apparel Through the Flat Pattern,* 6th ed. New York: Fairchild, 1992. Everything you always wanted to know about turning basic flat drafted patterns into any style imaginable.

Liechty, Elizabeth, Della Pottberg, and Judith Rasband. *Fitting and Pattern Alteration: A Multi-Method Approach.* New York: Fairchild, 1992. An exhaustive catalog of 85 figure variations, with three ways to adjust for each.

Pizzuto, J. J. *Fabric Science,* 6th ed. New York: Fairchild, 1994. Technical information on fibers, threads, knits and wovens, dyes, finishing, and textile laws.

Shaeffer, Claire. *Fabric Sewing Guide,* Rev. ed. Radnor, PA: Chilton, 1995. A comprehensive reference on fabrics; includes sewing tips.

resources

Equipment, Basic Sewing Supplies, and Tools

Interfacings, linings, and equipment

All Brands Sew-Knit-Serge & Embroidery, 9789 Florida Boulevard, Baton Rouge, LA 70815; (800) 739-7374. Web site: www.all-brands.com. Great prices and service for all kinds of new and refurbished sewing machines, sergers, irons, and all other kinds of sewing room equipment. They take trade-ins.

Atlanta Thread and Supply, 695 Red Oak Road, Stockbridge, GA 30281; (800) 847-1001. Equipment, linings, interfacings, tailoring supplies, and notions.

Greenberg and Hammer, 24 West 57th Street, New York, NY 10019-3918; (800) 955-5135. Linings, interfacings, tailoring supplies, and difficult-to-find notions.

Softwear Productions, 2523 S. Archer Avenue, Chicago, IL 60608; (800) 297-9670. Web site: www.softwearproductions.com; E-mail: softwear@rocketmail.com. Notions and linings, including Bemberg in 80 colors.

Dress forms and supplies

CSZ Enterprises, Inc., 1228 West 11th Street, #200, Tracy, CA 95376; (209) 832-4324. "My Twin" dress forms and pants forms, custom made or kits. Kit for plaster bandage body cast to be filled with insulation foam. No size limit.

Dress Rite Forms, 3817 N. Pulaski, Chicago, IL 60641; (773) 588-5761. Industrial forms with collapsible shoulders. Standard forms up to a 3X (53½–42½–54½), custom forms cast from plaster bandage technique in any size. $200 to $900. Dress Rite Gold Body Forms reproduce posture and proportions of women over 55; rounded upper back, lower bust, and they actually have a tummy! Standardized to a size 16; custom forms available.

National Business Products, 7165 KLM Oakland Mills Road, Columbia, MD 21046; (800) 875-8230. Sealing tape for paper tape dress forms. Product #USF2163, 2 in. by 600 ft. This size roll will make one dress form.

Uniquely You Dress Form. Custom muslin cover filled with foam, available to size large, maximum 51–44–50. Available through Atlanta Thread and Supply (see address on p. 149).

Hangers

Robert H. Ham Associates, P.O. Box 77398, Greensboro, NC 27417; (800) 334-6965. Web site: www.robertham.com; E-mail: sales@robertham.com. 18" and 19" hangers, foam hanger pads.

Undergarments

Springer Lingerie, 11230-B Grandview Avenue, Wheaton, MD 20902; (800)237-0065. Catalog. Sizes up to an I cup, 54-in. band. If they don't have what you need, they will find it for you.

Suzanne Henri, Absolute Perfection Bras, 111 Lee Grant Avenue, P.O. Box 2399, Appomattox, VA 24522; (800)634-2590. Bras and corsets. Specialize in plus and hard-to-find sizes.

Fabrics

Designer's Choice, P.O. Box 99, Belwood, PA 16617-0099; (800) 858-8522. Swatching service. Nice coordinates, good prices, mostly natural or breathable fibers.

G Street Portfolio, 12240 Wilkins Avenue, Rockville, MD 20852; (800) 333-9191. Swatching service. Mostly natural fibers, coordinates, nice quality, and selection. Moderate prices.

Hemp Traders, 2130 Colby Avenue, Suite #1, Los Angeles, CA 90025; (310) 914-9557. E-mail: hemptrader@aol.com. Swatches. Wholesale and retail; will dye to order. Every weight and weave from every international source imaginable; good prices.

Imaginations Mail Order Fabrics, 511 Penn Avenue, Sinking Spring, PA 19608; (800) 343-6953. Swatching service. An eclectic collection, include designer cuts, some coordinates, and mostly natural fibers. Fun and cheap.

Kieffers, P.O. Box 7500, Jersey City, NJ 07307; (201) 798-2266. Catalog. Lingerie fabric, swim wear fabrics, and findings. Inexpensive.

Oriental Silk Co., 8377 Beverly Boulevard, Los Angeles, CA 90048; (213) 651-2323. Swatches. All kinds of silks; also wool gabardine, crepe, linens. Good prices.

Sawyer Brook Distinctive Fabrics, P.O. Box 1800, Clinton, MA 01510; (800) 290-2739. Web site: www.ultranet.com/~sbdf; E-mail: sbdf@ultranet.com. Fine-quality, coordinated natural and breathable fibers in exquisite colorways. Linings, interfacings, buttons, and so on also available. Pricey, but well worth it.

Thai Silks, 252 State Street, Los Altos, CA 94022; (800) 722-SILK (in CA, 800-721-SILK). Swatches; fabric club. Great service, selection, prices.

Vogue Fabrics by Mail, 618 Hartrey Avenue, Evanston, IL 60202; (800) 433-4313. Nice quality natural fiber and synthetic coordinates. Moderate prices.

Patterns for Plus Sizes

I have grouped the following according to overall usefulness to plus-sized sewers.

These are primarily designed and graded for plus sizes. All or nearly all patterns are available in a wide range of larger sizes. Catalog or brochures are attractive and easy to understand. A wide variety of styles are available for a range of sewing expertise.

Burda Plus: Fashion for the Fuller Figure. Available from GLP International, 153 S. Dean Street, Englewood, NJ 07631; (800) 457-4443. Web site: Info@glpnews.com. Sizes for some patterns go up to 57½–50½–60. Annual, very attractive magazine that includes traceable patterns and instructions. You must trace each pattern piece over a color-coded "road map" on which all the pieces for all the three dozen or so patterns are printed; then you have to add seam and hem allowances. Styles are attractive, interestingly detailed, and worth the tedium of tracing. Metric.

Fashion Patterns by Coni, 2370 West Highway 89-a, Suite 11, Box 128, Sedona, AZ 86336; (520) 204-9362. Easy to sew, basic sportswear separates, including lined jackets and coats. Sizes 1X–7X, bust 44–66, waist 40–56, hips 48–70. Other sizes on request. Patterns are proportioned for height. Uses a unique grading system specifically designed for plus sizes.

Unique Patterns, 5670 Spring Garden Road, Suite 600, Halifax, NS (Canada) B3J IHG.; (800) 543-4739. E-mail: unique @ns.sympatico.ca. Custom-drafted patterns in unlimited sizes. Auto CAD driven. Newsletter, detailed measuring video provided; needs 43 measurements. Will adjust for figure variations and basic design variations. Over 100 styles, including basic, easy-to-sew sportswear, career-wear, and lingerie. Tested on up to 87-in. hips. Attractive catalog; nice service.

These do include plus sizes; they may include a smaller range of plus sizes; or they may be smaller collections or less intricate styles than those above.

Paw Prints Pattern Company, Purrfection Artistic Wearables, 19618 Canyon Drive, Granite Falls, WA 98252; (800) 691-4293. Web site: www.purrfection.com. Sizes up to 5X (62–54–64). A small collection of basic, easy-to-sew separates and some unique designs suitable for embellishment or wearable art. Also notions, rubber stamps for fabric printing, buttons.

Sewgrand, 1160 Yew Avenue, Bin 21, Blaine, WA 98321-8019, or 185-9040 Blundell Road, Suite 272, Richmond, BC V6Y 1K3, Canada; (604) 274-3274. Web site: www.sewgrand.com. Online catalog, or request by mail. Sizes 12–26, up to a 2X (50–42–52). Basic, simple-to-sew sportswear separates, many for slinkys.

The Sewing Workshop, 2010 Balboa Street, San Francisco, CA 94121; (800) 466-1599. Web site: www.sewingworkshop.com. Unique and exciting, origami-style designs for tops, pants, skirts, coats, and dresses. All designs run to an 18, many to a 22, but tops have plenty of ease.

Smaller, specialized collections or simpler designs

L. J. Designs, P.O. Box 2116, Reno, NV 89515-1116; (702) 853-2207. Web site: www.sewnet.com/ljdesigns; E-mail: LYLA777 @aol.com. A small collection of simple, easy-to-sew sportswear separates and some unique designs up to a 28 (50–43–53).

Patterns for Every Body: Designs That Flatter, 18476 Prospect Road, Saratoga, CA 95070; (800) 587-3937. A small collection of patterns up to a XXL (52¾–45½–54½).

Peggy Sagers, 305 Spring Creek Village, #326, Dallas, TX 75248; (800) 784-8245. Sizes up to XL (51–43–53). Graded for plus-sized proportions, and sized by "industrial standards." Ready-to-wear–style sportswear separates, including lined jacket. Patterns are adjustable for up to a D cup size. Instructions use industrial techniques.

Scrubs by Mail, 504 E Gemini Drive, Tempe, AZ 85283; (800) 332-1582. Several designs up to a 5X (bust 64, hips 65), for medical personnel; also fabrics, notions, and kits for scrubs.

Stretch and Sew, P.O. Box 25306, Tempe AZ 85285-5306; (800) 547-7717. Web site: www.stretch-and-sew.com; E-mail: stretch-sew@worldnet.alt.net; Easy-to-sew sportswear, mostly styles up to 1X (46–38–48), and many up to 3X (56–48–58).

Professional Organization

The Professional Association of Custom Clothiers (PACC), P.O. Box 8071, Medford, OR 97504-0071; (541)772-4119. Web site: www.paccprofessionals.org. Contact for referrals to local sewing professionals.

index

Note: Italics indicate a photograph or illustration.